With a fine feeling for
FOOD

With a fine feeling for
FOOD

Selected and tested traditional Scots recipes

JANET MURRAY

Impulse Books

Aberdeen

First published 1972
by Impulse Publications Limited
28 Guild Street
Aberdeen
Scotland

I offer this work to the memory of
the late Lord Boyd Orr and to Lady
Boyd Orr in loving and grateful
appreciation for their unfailing help
and encouragement in my efforts to
keep alive our very fine tradition
in Scots cookery.

Printed in Scotland by the Aberdeen
University Press Ltd. on Glastonbury
Coloured Antique Laid Paper

CONTENTS

Children making toffee 1878

Illustrated with line drawings and 19th century advertisements from the collection at the Mary Evans Picture Library.

INTRODUCTION

With a fine feeling for food I have selected and tested Scots recipes, many of which have been familiar to me since childhood.

From thirty years of experience of writing on the subject of Scots dishes, first in the *Glasgow Herald,* then in the *Farming News* and *Scotland Magazine,* latterly speaking on the air, I find that readers and listeners alike appreciate having one recipe pinpointed in preference to having to choose from many and, because of this, I have given what I have found to be the best recipe for each particular dish.

It has been my great good fortune over the years to have been given many 'personal' recipes; by this I mean family favourites which have lost their original identity and have become known as 'Mary's recipe', or 'Grandma's pudding'. In almost all such cases the recipes are very good indeed.

I have included a few for their interest, such as a cream cheese made in a cow's bladder, a gigot of mutton roasted on a clock-work jack, sowens and the preparing of rennet.

JANET MURRAY

Soups

Soup: The Food Value

If there are vegetables in the soup then their mineral salts will be in it as well as some vitamins. Barley, for instance, has lime, phosphates, iron and fat; some root vegetables—carrots, parsnips, and beet—contain sugar; peas, beans and lentils contain a large proportion of protein; potatoes and rice are full of starch which, in the process of digestion, is changed into a simple form of sugar.

If there is a bone in the soup pot there will be just enough fat in the soup to be beneficial without it being greasy and unpalatable.

So there are mineral salts, protein, fat and some vitamins in your plate of soup.

The Stock Pot

Odds and ends of meat trimmings, bacon rinds, giblets and bones should go into a stock pot and be cooked long and slowly.

All liquid in which meat, fish, game, poultry or vegetables like celery, peas, cauliflower and carrots have been cooked should also go into the stock pot.

Never leave stock in the pot overnight. Strain it and leave it in as cool a place as possible.

Flavouring

The cooks of other days were bold and adventurous in their use of flavouring: herbs, peppercorns, cloves, almost always a few grains of sugar, curry powder, relish and a wide range of vegetables were used as well as culinary colourings.

Large brown earthenware cooking pots used to sit at the side of the cooking range, simmering away for a day, giving off a most delicious aroma when the lid was lifted.

Rice, barley flour, and even a handful of Scottish oatmeal was used for thickening, and grated cheese was often added.

Attention was also paid to colour: most cooks made their own browning and caramel. A green pea soup would certainly have a little green colouring added and a slice of beetroot was a favourite for colouring tomato soup.

All soups are clearer and sweeter if skimmed occasionally during the cooking.

The Aul' Wife's Soup

A piece of celery	1 pint water
2 large onions	1 pint milk
6 potatoes	A wee suppie cream
A bunch of parsley	Pepper and salt
1 oz butter	

Parboil and slice the onions, cut the celery into pieces, peel and slice the potatoes and wash the parsley.

Heat the butter in the soup pot, and lightly toss the onions and the celery in it. Add the potatoes, the parsley, the seasoning and the water.

Boil until the vegetables are cooked then put the soup through a sieve.

Return to the pot, add the milk and bring to the boil. Add more seasoning if necessary. Pour the cream into the tureen; then pour the soup on top of it.

Cabbage Soup: Miss Mary's

A good sized cabbage	2 pints milk
1 onion	Cupful of cream
Piece of butter (the size of	Pepper, salt and chopped
a small egg)	parsley

Have a large pan of boiling water on the fire. Wash the cabbage and pick it over most carefully before shredding it finely.

Place it in the pan and boil quickly for 5 minutes. Empty the contents of the pan into a strainer, and put the butter into the hot pan.

Slice the onion thinly and then chop it finely. Brown it lightly in the butter then toss the strained cabbage in the butter. Season, add the milk and the same quantity of water, and boil gently for 30 minutes.

Add the chopped parsley and the cream at the last minute and serve with oatcakes and boiled potatoes.

Carrot Soup

1 quart stock
3 large carrots
2 oz butter or margarine
2 pints milk

4 oz flour
Pepper, salt and chopped
  parsley

Wash, scrape and cut the carrots into slices. Cook them in the stock until they are tender and then rub them through a sieve.

Melt the butter in the pan and add the flour stirring it well over a gentle heat.

Add the milk slowly, stirring all the time, until you have a smooth creamy sauce which should be cooked for about 5 minutes. Then add the carrot puree slowly, season to taste and colour a little with cochineal.

Put the chopped parsley into the tureen and pour the soup over it.

Cream of Celery

1 quart stock
½ pint milk
1 head celery

Yolks of 2 eggs
Pepper, salt and a little grated
  onion

Wash the celery thoroughly and cut it into small pieces. Cook it and the onion in the stock until tender. (Chicken stock is delicious with celery but not essential.)

Put it through a sieve and return it to the pan. Season it to taste and add a few grains of sugar.

Bring to the boil and add the milk. Take it aside and let it go just off the boil.

Beat the egg yolks in the soup tureen, slowly add a little of the soup, beating vigorously the while. Gradually add all the soup and serve at once.

Cockie-leekie

This is a very old recipe which includes oatmeal:

2 quarts 'hen bree' (chicken stock)	A cupful of cream
4 to 6 leeks (according to size)	Pepper, salt and chopped parsley
1 oz oatmeal	

Wash and slice the leeks thinly and add them to the boiling stock; add the oatmeal blended with a little cold water; season and cook until the leeks are tender. Skim if necessary.

Put the cream and the parsley into the tureen and pour the boiling soup over them.

Cockie-leekie with Rice

An old fowl was used for this and, since an old bird is often very fat, it is wise to boil the bird in ample water first. Skim frequently and if this does not succeed in getting most of the fat off, strain through a piece of fine linen which will *kep* (hold back) the grease.

Wash and trim some leeks: do not use a great deal of the green part. It is difficult to give a quantity of leeks as they differ so much in size, but about 1 lb finely cut is enough for the stock of one bird.

Bring the stock to the boil and put in the prepared leeks and two tablespoonfuls of whole rice. Boil for 30 minutes, skimming if necessary. Cut some of the white meat into small pieces and put them into the tureen. Pour the hot soup over them and serve at once.

Some cooks liked to add a few well cooked and slightly sweetened prunes to cockie-leekie just before dishing.

Crowdie (1)

The traditional crowdie was a batter-like mixture of sour milk, or buttermilk, and oatmeal and was eaten at breakfast. Later it widened in scope and was eaten as a main meal made with a stock from fowl, beef or just a bone.

The following recipe is a Dundee recipe published in a cookery book, dated 1804.

Save the liquor in which you have cooked hen, mutton or beef as long as it is not salt beef. Bring to the boil and stir in two *neivefuls* (handfuls) of fine oatmeal, stirring with vigour until the whole is well to the boil.

Serve with boiled potatoes.

Crowdie (2)

This recipe and the following are in a cookery book published in 1878.

Put 2 gallons of any meat liquor, either fresh or salt, free from all fat, into a large goblet. Bring well nigh to boiling point. Mix in ½ pint of oatmeal with cold water, add two large or a dozen small onions cut up as small as the oatmeal, a good shake of pepper and a teaspoonful of sugar.

Add salt according to need (if the liquor is from salt beef, no salt will be needed). Boil for 30 minutes.

Crowdie (3)

4 oz pot barley	4 oz oatmeal
4 oz sliced onion	5 quarts of good stock, beef or
2 oz of a good dripping	chicken
4 oz bacon	

Wash the barley and let it soak in cold water for 24 hours. Just cover so that it will drink most of the water.

Cook it with the stock and the onion until the barley is soft (about 2 hours).

About ¾ of an hour before meal time put the dripping into a pot, let it become fairly hot then fry the bacon in it until crisp.

Stir in the oatmeal until it has soaked up most of the fat, then slowly add the boiling stock. Add plenty of pepper and salt if required and let it boil for 30 minutes.

Cullen Skink

This is a fish soup with potatoes in it. It can be made with white fish but is tastiest when made with a finnan haddock, skin, bones and lugs, but 1 lb of yellow fillet does very well. If you do use a whole finnan haddock, cook it, then remove it from the stock to skin and bone it and then return the flesh to the stock.

1 lb boneless yellow fillet of fish	1 pint milk
6 large potatoes	4 pints water
1 onion	Pepper, salt, and a few grains of sugar

Cook the fillet in the water with the potatoes sliced, the onion cut small and the seasoning. When the potatoes are cooked break up the fish and potatoes with a whisk. Add the milk and bring almost to boiling point.

Just before serving add a knob of butter.

Curried Soup

This is a soup definitely requiring fish stock.

4 pints fish stock	1 tablespoonful curry powder
1 large onion	1 tablespoonful curry paste
1 green apple	Pepper and salt
A bunch of parsley	2 oz butter
A knob of root ginger	4 oz whole rice

Use a cod's head and some fish trimmings to make the stock; strain it.

Slice the apple and the onion and fry them lightly in the butter, but do not let them brown. Add the stock, parsley, the root ginger, slightly bruised with the tattie chapper, and cook for 1 hour.

Strain it, return it to the pan and add the curry powder blended with a little water, the curry paste and the rice, well washed. Cook until the rice is tender, usually between twenty and thirty minutes.

Season to taste, and add a little sugar if you feel it can stand it.

Fife Broth

Ask your butcher to save you some bare ribs of pork. Soak a cupful of barley overnight, then put on the ribs, barley and pepper and salt with plenty of water.

Cook gently for about 2 hours, then add a large onion finely chopped and a dozen raw potatoes peeled and sliced. Cook another 30 minutes and when ready serve with oatcakes.

Fish Soup

3 pints fish stock	A bunch of parsley
1 pint milk	Salt
1 onion	A cupful of cream
6 peppercorns	2 tablespoonfuls flour

Put the fish stock into a soup pot. Add the onion, peppercorns, parsley and salt. Cook gently for 30 minutes and then strain. Return the stock to the pot, add the milk and bring almost to boiling point.

Blend the flour smoothly with a little cold water and pour a ladleful of the stock over it, mix it well and add to the stock. Bring it through the boil and add the cream.

Putting a little of the stock to the blended flour instead of putting the blend right into the pot keeps it from lumping.

A Useful Fish Stock

1 lb good fish trimmings	1 sprig of rosemary
1 quart water	Onion, carrot, celery and parsley
1 blade of mace	Salt and pepper

Bring to the boil, cook gently for 30 minutes and strain.

If you like garlic a tiny piece is a decided improvement. This can be used for a fish soup, for a fish sauce or to help in the making of a fish forcemeat.

Anchovy essence can be added as a colouring or as a flavouring.

Game Soup: The Old Boy's

Prepare one partridge, two pigeons, a pheasant and an old boiling hen for cooking. Slice off the breast of the pheasant and the hen. Wash well two hare legs.

Shred a moderate sized cabbage and a head of celery. Allow a dozen leeks, unless they are too large, but do not use too much of the green part.

Put the meat and six cloves, a dozen black peppercorns, and salt into about 6 pints of water and bring slowly to the boil, skimming as it does so. Cook for 1 hour continuing to skim from time to time.

Add the vegetables, boil up again and skim. *Now* add a marrow bone and put the lid on the pot. No more skimming is required. When the meat is coming freely from the bones strain the stock. Pick the meat from the bones and put it through a not too fine mincer.

Rub the stock pot quite vigorously with a clove of garlic and melt a lump of butter in it. Bring to sizzling and toss a good cupful of oatmeal in the butter until pale brown. Now slowly add the stock and boil for 30 minutes; then add the minced meat and more seasoning if necessary. Wine can be added but personally I do not recommend it.

Make a dish for another day with the breasts.

Duck Soup: Farmhouse

Allow a couple of ducks to 6
pints water
Add
1 carrot
A piece of turnip

3 onions
Half a head of celery
4 potatoes
A bunch of parsley
Pepper, salt and browning

Prepare the ducks for the pot and cook them with all the ingredients for 30 minutes after coming to the boil, skimming well during that time. Then add a large marrow bone and skim no further as the delicate globules of marrow fat are a delicacy.

When the birds are very tender, lift them from the pot. Put the soup through a hair sieve but do not rub through any of the vegetables. Return the stock to the pot. Cut the meat off the birds and chop finely. (Do *not* use a mincer.)

Give the meat a dust of salt and pepper and add to the stock. Bring to the boil and no more. Taste it and add more salt or pepper if necessary.

Draw to the side of the fire and add orange juice to taste (about ½ a pint).

Serve with boiled potatoes.

Hare Soup (Bawd Bree)

Some inferior parts of a hare
2 oz good dripping
Onion, carrot, turnip and a
piece of celery
4 whole cloves

A dozen peppercorns
Salt
2 large tablespoons flour
4 quarts water

Cut the parts of hare into small pieces, wash and dry. Heat the dripping in a soup pot. Add the pieces of hare and some sliced onion and brown them slowly. Add the other vegetables, pour in the water and add the seasoning. (Use warm water for preference.)

Bring to the boil, and cook slowly for 3 hours. Season to taste with salt after an hour's cooking.

Now rub the meat through a sieve, strain the stock and put both meat and stock back in the pan. Skim well to remove any surplus fat.

Blend the flour with cold water and add some of the warm stock to it; then pour it into the stock. Stir until it comes to the boil, boil for 5 minutes, taste again for seasoning and add a glass of port wine.

The soup can be served now but for those who like it the blood of the hare is considered a delicacy that must be added to the soup.

Assuming that you have kept the blood, see that it is free from clots and put it in a roomy basin. Slowly add some of the soup to it, beating it well with a wire beater or a slotted spoon. Have the soup very hot, but not boiling, and stir in the blood. On no account let it boil after this.

In some parts of Scotland a black pudding is skinned and sliced into the soup.

Plain boiled potatoes are always served with hare soup.

Hare Soup without Blood

This is an old Scots harvest recipe and can be cut to suit individual tastes.

1 hare	Large bunch parsley
2 lb boiling beef and marrow bone	12 peppercorns
	6 cloves, salt
1 gallon water	Some good dripping
3 large onions	A large bowl of soft white
1 large head celery	bread crumbs
3 carrots	2 gills port
Piece of turnip	

Cut the hare into smallish joints and wash and dry them well. Prepare all the vegetables, slicing the onions thinly.

Heat the dripping in the soup pot and fry the onion and joints of hare. When these are lightly browned add the water (fairly hot if possible) and the beef and skim until it comes to the boil. Add all the other ingredients except the breadcrumbs and the port.

Cook gently for 3 hours—longer if the hare is old. Lift out the joints, remove the flesh from the bones and mince it. Set aside the boiled beef, strain the stock and return it to the pot. Add the minced hare and the breadcrumbs and bring almost to the boil.

Just before lifting add the port wine.

Hotch-Potch

1½ lb shoulder of mutton	diced carrot, turnip, cauli-
2½ quarts water	flower
4 spring onions, sliced	A small lettuce, shredded
1 pint green peas	Parsley, chopped
1 pint broad beans	Pepper and salt
1½ gills each of prepared and	

Boil the mutton in the water, skimming occasionally. Let it cook for two hours, then add all the vegetables except the parsley. Season and boil for another hour; skim. Take out the meat, remove it from the bone and cut it into little pieces before returning it to the pot.

Season to taste and add the chopped parsley before serving.

Hough Soup

1 lb hough	1 turnip (or a piece if large)
2 quarts water	A teacupful of sago
1 large onion	Pepper and salt
1 carrot	

Put the hough on with the water and the vegetables cut up roughly. Cook gently, skimming occasionally, until the meat is tender.

Strain the stock and return it to the pot. Wash the sago in cold water and put it into the stock. Stir until it comes to the boil. Season with pepper and salt and cook until the sago is transparent.

Meanwhile cut the meat from the bone and add it just before serving.

Serve with boiled potatoes.

Kidney Soup

5 pints stock	Pepper, salt and a little browning
½ lb kidney	A dessertspoonful of good
1 large onion	dripping
2 tablespoonfuls flour	

Wash the kidney and dry it on a clean towel. Cut it into tiny pieces, remove any fatty core and toss it in flour seasoned with pepper and salt. Melt the dripping in a warm soup pot, add the kidney and fry gently until brown.

Remove the kidney. Fry the onion well. Replace the kidney, add the stock and bring to the boil. Skim the soup occasionally, and let it boil for 2½ hours.

Blend the flour with a little lukewarm water in a roomy bowl. Add two ladlefuls of soup to this blend and then pour it into the soup. Add more salt and pepper if necessary, and enough browning to make it a colourful brown.

Note: More kidney can be used if a more meaty soup is desired.

Milk Broth

This belongs to the days when the pot hung on the *swee* and *hottered* away all morning (morning beginning about five o'clock).

Barley requires long cooking but long soaking does away with some of the cooking time.

For 2 pints of milk allow 2 oz pot barley which has been soaked in a pint of water for 24 hours.

To make the broth put the barley and the water in which it has been soaking into a saucepan. If the water has been absorbed make it up to the pint again. Let this cook slowly for an hour, then add the milk. Bring it to the boil and cook gently until the barley is soft. Add pepper and salt and put in a cupful of cream just before serving.

Oatcakes should be served with milk broth.

Lentil Split Pea Soup

4 to 6 oz lentils or split peas to a quart of water

Stock is not essential but a good marrow bone, a ham bone, or even ham trimmings, make a delicious soup.

Split peas are better soaked in cold water overnight and lentils must be well washed. Almost any vegetable goes with this soup but an onion and a piece of celery are essential. Lentil or split pea soup can be eaten unsieved in which case vegetables should be diced. If you prefer to sieve the soup the vegetables can be cooked in lumps and put through the sieve.

A teaspoonful of chopped mint added after the sieving is an old method of flavouring this soup.

Lang Kail

This is a good old Scots dish, very satisfying and eaten like soup.

Strip a pailful of curly green kail and wash the blades well. Put them into a roomy pan with boiling water, well salted. (You do not need a lot of water). Do not over-cook, and, if anything, drain off the water while the kail is still underdone. Put a good lump of butter into the pot, put on the lid and finish the cooking in a gentle heat.

Chop the kail as you would mash potatoes, season with pepper and salt and add a handful of oatmeal. Stir it all well, and at the last minute pour in a cupful of cream or good milk.

Mushroom Broth: Colonel Cameron's

A bowl of mushrooms
A piece of boiling mutton, neck, shanks or spare ribs
4 oz pot barley
A piece of carrot, turnip and parsnip
4 oz leeks
Salt, pepper, a snifter of sugar

Soak the barley overnight and wash it well. Let it boil for 3 hours in a pot with a gallon of water and the boiling mutton, cooking gently. Skim from time to time. Remove the meat.

Meanwhile dice the carrot, turnip, parsnip, peel the mushrooms and cut them into small pieces. The leeks must be shorn finely. Add all this to the pot and bring to the boil again.

Boil gently and skim occasionally, season to taste and allow to cook until the vegetables are tender (about $\frac{3}{4}$ of an hour).

Partan Bree (Crab Soup) (1)

Take two cooked crabs and pull them into pieces. Reserve the flesh from the claws and put all the other edible parts into a stockpot along with some good fish trimmings, a blade of mace, an onion, and some parsley and add four pints of water. Cook for 30 minutes. (Long cooking is neither advisable nor necessary). Strain the stock into a basin, measure it and return it to the pan.

Bring to the boil, add 4 oz of whole rice and cook until the rice is tender. Season as required, then add the meat from the claws cut in sizeable pieces. Put a cup of milk or cream into the soup tureen, add some finely chopped parsley and ladle the partan bree on top of it.

Serve with boiled potatoes.

Partan Bree (Crab Soup) (2)

2 cooked crabs	Pepper and salt
1 cod's head	Anchovy sauce
1 onion	1 pint milk
1 gill cream	3 oz whole rice

Cook the cod's head and the onion in enough water to give 1 pint of stock; strain it, reserving any pieces of fish. Take all the edible parts from the crab, setting aside the meat from the large claws.

Return the fish stock to the pan, and boil the rice in it until it is very well cooked. Add the meat from the head, the meat from the body of the crab and anchovy sauce to taste.

Season with salt and pepper to taste and rub through a sieve. Return to the pan, bring to the boil, add the milk, heat again but not quite through the boil. Add the cream just before serving, along with the chopped meat from the large claws.

Ox Tail Soup

This is one of the most satisfying of soups but to be perfect the tail must be perfectly cooked, which takes time.

Cut the tail into joints and trim off most of the fat. Whether for soup or for a stew it is really an improvement to parboil ox tail. Bring the joints in a pan of cold water slowly to the boil. Strain off all the water. Put a piece of butter or good dripping into the soup pot and bring it almost to boiling point.

Put in the joints making sure that they are quite dry or the fat will spit. Brown the joints. Fry one large onion cut very small along with them then add the water, a piece of carrot, turnip and celery and stick two cloves in the carrot. Let this come to the boil and allow it to cook gently for 3 hours.

Some of the smaller pieces may be cooked before the bigger pieces, if so take them out.

When the soup is about ready remove the pieces of vegetables, thicken it with 2 tablespoonfuls of flour, add pepper and salt and a little browning. Bring through the boil again and serve with the joints of tail in it.

Potato Soup (1)

Potato soup is never sweeter than when made with a marrow bone.

Boil the bone in about a quart of water with 6 medium-sized potatoes, a leek finely sliced and 1 carrot grated. Season with pepper, salt and a little celery salt and cook for 1 hour. The fat from a marrow bone is a light delicate fat and does not need to be skimmed off.

It used to be the custom to serve oatcakes with potato soup.

Potato Soup (2)

6 large potatoes	A piece of turnip
2 onions	A piece of celery
4 oz butter	A cup of cream
1 carrot	Pepper, salt and chopped parsley

Wash, peel and cut up the potatoes into small pieces. Peel and chop the onion. Shred the carrot and turnip and cut the celery into thin slices. Heat the butter in the soup pot, but do not let it brown.

Add the onions and cook them a little in the butter but again do not let them brown. Stir in all the other vegetables, tossing them well in the butter; add pepper and salt and fill the pot with enough warm water to cover the vegetables. Bring to the boil and cook for an hour.

Put the cream and the chopped parsley into the tureen and pour the boiling soup over them.

Sheep's Head Broth

At one time the blacksmith was taught the art of singeing a sheep's head and trotters. The head was impaled through the nostril on a poker and the head was moved back and fore over the smiddy fire until all the rough wool was burned off. Then the head was rubbed with a hot iron until it was 'black's the lum'. It was then split open and the brains were spread over it to whiten it. This brought the head back almost to its natural colour and after a good soaking it was ready for the broth pot.

The trotters were treated in the same way except that they were held by the 'taings' or tongs. The word used for this operation was 'sung' and the smith referred to as the 'singer'. The fee for a head and trotters was threepence.

Sheep's head broth has been called the king of Scotch broths and the following recipe is nearly two hundred years old.

Procure the head of a good wether with the four trotters and send them to the smiddy to be sung, or do it yourself and save a copper. Wash the head well, howk out the eyes, scraping the cavities with a sharp pointed knife.

Put the head and trotters into a pail of well water and add a large handful of salt and a spoonful of soda. Let them steep all night. Next day wash them well, scraping away any black or hairy bits.

Now put on the muckle pot with a gallon of water, put in the head and trotters and bring to the boil. Skim as often as may be necessary. Put in ½ lb of green peas, ½ lb pot barley well washed and much the same weight each of carrot, turnip and onion all cut up small. Half a dozen leeks should be well shorn and added along with shredded cabbage blades and last a cup of chopped parsley.

Season to taste with plenty of black pepper and salt. Add a few chunks of carrot and turnip to eat with the head. Skim frequently until the head and trotters are tender. Dish the soup in a tureen and put the head and trotters on an ashet with the carrot and turnip neatly about them.

White face sheep are said to boil more tenderly than blackfaced wethers, but the latter, in our opinion, make the finer broth.

Scotch Broth made with a Sheep's Head

6 pints water
2 oz barley
2 oz dried green peas
2 oz yellow split peas
A carrot, a piece of turnip

Some leek, a few blades of
  cabbage
A few blades of kail
A parsnip and some parsley
1 sheep's head

Soak the head overnight in cold, well salted water. Wash the green and yellow peas and the barley and cover with cold water overnight. Put the head in a roomy pot, cover it well with water and bring to the boil, skimming frequently. Now add the peas and barley. Cook this, again skimming occasionally, for 1½ hours. Add all the other vegetables diced, and cook for another 1½ hours.

Season with pepper and salt and add chopped parsley at the last minute.

Cream of Tomato Soup

2 lb tin tomatoes
1½ pints milk
2 oz butter
3 tablespoonfuls flour

Pepper, salt, a saltspoonful of
  sugar and the same amount
  bicarbonate of soda

Melt the butter in a roomy saucepan, add the flour and cook a little, stirring all the time. Add the milk slowly and go on stirring until the sauce is cooked.

Heat the contents of the tin of tomatoes and strain them. Add the bicarbonate of soda to the puree and slowly add it to the sauce. Season to taste, add more sugar if necessary and bring the soup almost to boiling point. Do not let it come right through the boil.

Serve at once.

Tomato Soup

1 quart tin tomatoes
Onion, carrot, sprig of parsley
3 pints stock

Pepper, salt, sugar
2 tablespoonfuls cornflour

Put all the ingredients into a saucepan, except the cornflour and sugar; bring to the boil and cook gently for 1 hour.

Strain the whole through a sieve and return to the pan. Season with pepper, salt and sugar to taste, and thicken with the cornflour blended with a little warm water.

Fish

Scottish Fisherwife's Cry

Caller Herrin'   *Fresh Herring*
Fine short dilse   *Dilse, a seaweed*
Pepper dilse and batheryochs *Two kinds of seaweed*
Partan taes an' raans.   *Crab claws and fish roes.*

Fish

The story of fish is far older than that of man himself, and geologists, who judge by fossils in rock, estimate that there were fish in existence some three hundred million years ago. Biblical references bring them much nearer and we know that the Roman epicures set much store by fish.

Britain being surrounded by the sea is, of course, deeply involved in fishing and its allied industries. In Scotland certain towns have given their names to smoked fish—the Aberdeen haddock, the Findon haddock, the Arbroath smokie, the Auchmithie smokie, and Collieston speldings.

Salt fish such as dried cod and herring in brine were once part of the staple diet in Scotland. Cod, haddock and hake were pickled and dried and sold dry. Oily fish like herring and mackerel were brine salted or pickled.

Red herrings were herrings pickled in brine for some days and then smoked; bloaters are herrings smoke cured after only a few hours in brine. Kippers are herring split down the back, run through pickle and then smoked. Buckling is a herring cooked and smoked in one operation.

Findon in Kincardineshire was the first village to smoke haddock which became known as a finnan haddock. The haddock was beheaded, split open and cleaned. Arbroath smokies are whole haddock smoked and can be eaten straight from the 'sticks' (the spars on which they are hung during smoking). Collieston speldings were haddock or whiting cleaned, split open and dried in the sun. Salmon used to be kippered and moulds for kippering salmon were to be found in most 'big houses'.

Fish should be as fresh as possible and in season: rigidity and stiffness of flesh is a good guide to the condition of fish and the smell should be pleasant. All fish should be cleaned quickly, without much handling and should never be left lying in water. After washing they should be dried on a clean towel.

Turbot fins are considered a delicacy and on no account must scales be scraped off salmon. This lordly fish goes to the pot with the minimum of trimming.

Boiling Fish

Large fish, or cuts of large fish, are best for boiling purposes, small fish being more suitable for frying, steaming or baking.

Have a large pan of boiling salted water ready, the salt in the proportion of one tablespoonful to a gallon of water. A spoonful of vinegar is an improvement if the fish is white, but not if you wish to use the stock for sauce or soup.

Lower the fish into the water, bring it back to boiling point again, and keep it at boiling point until the fish is cooked. It is not necessary to keep the water boiling vigorously.

Weigh the fish before putting it into the pan and then allow 10 minutes for every pound and 10 minutes over. If the fish is rather thick, use a fork to test it at the thickest end. If the flesh comes away cleanly from the bone it is ready. A fish so cooked should be full of juice and care must be taken when lifting it out lest it is broken and the juices lost.

Steaming Fish

If you do not have a pet steamer, this is an excellent method of steaming fish.

Butter a soup plate, put the fish on the plate, sprinkle with pepper and salt and tiny pieces of butter about the size of peas. Cover with buttered paper and put the plate on a pan of boiling water. Place the lid of the pan on top of the plate and let it steam for 30 minutes.

Fish Roe

Tie the required weight of fish roe in a piece of muslin. Have a pan of water at boiling point, add salt, bearing in mind the size of the roe, and a few drops of vinegar. Lower the roe into the pan and boil until it is set. A large piece of roe takes an hour to cook.

If it is to be eaten hot serve at once with a mustard sauce.

If cold, press it under a weight and cut in slices when cold. Alternatively egg and crumb the slices, or use the oatmeal coating, or dip in a good batter and fry in deep fat at boiling point.

Serve with anchovy sauce, slices of lemon and fried parsley.

Frying Fish

Almost every kind of fish is suitable for frying; small fish are fried whole while large fish can be cut in slices or filleted. Frying is a popular method of cooking but there is a fine distinction between frying and stewing not always realised. Fried fish should be brown and crisp, but if the fat has not been at the right temperature the result is a form of stewing and makes the fish soggy and greasy.

The fish should be quite dry no matter what coating is to be used. Whole fish or pieces of fish should be of uniform size. Use dried breadcrumbs or fine oatmeal to coat the fish. Put the crumbs or oatmeal on a piece of kitchen paper and season with pepper and salt. Beat an egg thoroughly and dip the fish in this using a brush but do not overload with egg. Dip the fish in the crumbs, patting them in to coat them evenly.

For frying use a saucepan with enough fat or oil to cover the fish or a frying basket if you have one. Let the fat come to the boil: if it splutters there is water in it but this evaporates as it heats. When the fat is still and a faint blue smoke rises put in the fish.

Do not put too many pieces in at once as this will lower the temperature too much. Cook until the fish is brown and firm; the time required varies according to the thickness of the fish. Lift the basket clear of the fat, let it drip for a few minutes, then turn the fish on to a hot plate covered with kitchen paper. Fish can also be coated with batter before frying.

Always bring the fat back to boiling point before putting in a second frying.

Grilling White Fish

The art of grilling white fish is to cook it slowly and to keep it moist and juicy. Small fish such as whiting, dabs and sole can be grilled whole but larger fish such as cod or halibut must be filleted or cut in slices.

Season with pepper and salt and then brush with melted butter or with a good cooking oil. Scatter a little grated lemon rind over it and arrange on the bottom of a well oiled grill pan. Grill slowly, turning the fish and brushing again with oil or butter.

When ready the fish should be lightly browned and the flesh leave the bone easily.

Fish Garnishes

Lemon in thick slices or in quarters
Parsley fried, chopped or sprig
Slices of hard-boiled egg
Yolks of hard-boiled eggs put through a fine sieve

Tomatoes, skinned, sliced and seasoned with salt, pepper, a dust of sugar and a few drops of olive oil
Chives, parsley, fennel and chervil

A Stuffing for Fish

2 oz fine white breadcrumbs
1 oz butter
Salt, pepper, a suspicion of nutmeg grated

A teaspoonful of chopped parsley
A little grated lemon rind
Bind together with beaten egg

Finnan Haddock: Mary Annie's Method

Cut the haddock into portions and cook gently in a saucepan with enough milk to cover them. Add pepper (salt if needed) and a shake of celery salt. While the haddock is cooking—and it will not take long—take a piece of butter about the size of a small egg and work as much flour into it as it will take.

Lift the haddock on to a warm ashet, take the pan away from the fire, and drop in the ball of buttered flour. With a fork beat until it is smooth and put back on the fire to come through the boil.

Serve the sauce in a warmed sauceboat.

Finnan Haddock: Jessie's Jeems' Favourite

Take a 'wise-like' (decent size) finnan haddock and give it a trim. Dip it in flour and cover it well. Fry it slowly in a spoonful of good dripping, then put in a cupful of milk and a good shake of black pepper.

Put a lid on the pan and cook the fish slowly until it comes clean from the bone.

('Jessie's Jeems' is a 'tee' name, a form of identification used in fishing villages where there are very few who are not of the same surname).

Finnan Haddock Roly-Poly

1 lb finnan haddock	2 eggs
8 to 12 potatoes	Pepper, a little salt and some
1 tablespoonful thick cream or	chopped parsley
a piece of butter	

Take a pound of finnan haddock, cooked, skinned and free from bone.

Boil the potatoes and shake them very dry. Mash them thoroughly until they are quite smooth, then add the cream or the butter (but not both).

Season, being very cautious with the salt in case the fish is salty.

Stir in the fish, not too finely flaked, and then the well beaten eggs, and the parsley. Add a good shake of pepper and taste for salt.

Flouring the hands, shape the mixture into a roly and brush over with beaten egg. Roll firmly in brown breadcrumbs. Bake in a hot oven for 30 minutes, until brown and crisp.

Seasoning for Fish

½ lb white pepper	¼ oz cayenne
½ oz grated nutmeg	1 teaspoonful salt
¼ oz ground mace	1 teaspoonful fine sugar

Put through a fine sieve twice and bottle and cork well.

Cod Sounds

Cod sounds were salted in quantity and like salt fish had to be mellowed before cooking. The mellow was water, or milk and water, or skimmed milk. The favourite method of cooking was a slow boiling until tender and dressing with a cheese sauce.

Jugged Kippers

Have a deep earthenware pot on the stove but not on direct heat, and almost fill with boiling water. Hang the kippers over a long spoon or spurtle across the top of the pot, tied in pairs by the tail so that they are immersed in the water. Cover with a thickness of flannel and leave for 30 minutes.

No further cooking. Dry well and glaze with butter.

A Scots Fish Coating

Break an egg on a plate large enough to take the fish. Beat thoroughly with a knife. Season sufficient fine oatmeal with pepper and salt and a pinch of nutmeg and put it on an ashet or a piece of clean kitchen paper.

Brush each fish or fillet of fish so that it is evenly coated with egg without being runny.

Then dip them in the oatmeal which should be patted on to give a good coating.

This makes an excellent coating for fish which are to be fried and gives them flavour.

Herring

Today very few people buy herring on the bone, but the gourmet does like to bone his own herring. Herring should be unbroken, of a silvery-green colour and well covered with scales. Avoid a great deal of handling. Cut off the head, the tail and the fins, remove the gut and scrape off as much of the scales as possible then wash the herring in very cold water. To bone a herring, use the thumb to free the bone from the flesh and take away with the backbone as many of the smaller bones as you can.

Fried Herring

Have the herring cleaned, boned and dried on a clean towel. Put a handful of fine oatmeal on a plate and season it well with pepper and salt. Dip the herring in this coating, covering them well, back and front.

Have a frying pan with some hot fat in it (a lot of fat is unnecessary), put the herring in back first, and fry for 3 to 5 minutes, depending on the thickness of the fish. Turn them and give them the same cooking on the other side. They should be a light brown and very crisp when ready.

Grilled Herring

Do not bone the fish but have them well scaled and very dry. Make two incisions crosswise on both sides with a very sharp knife and brush them with melted butter well seasoned with pepper and salt. Cook them not too quickly under a hot grill—time according to size—and baste occasionally with the melted seasoned butter.

Stuffed Herring

Firm unbroken fish of a uniform size are required for this. Wash, scale and dry the herrings. With a very sharp knife make a cut down the back from head to tail leaving both head and tail on. Free the bone and remove it. Cut and remove any black skin.

For 6 large herring season 4 oz of fine oatmeal with pepper and salt and a shake of celery salt; add some finely chopped parsley and a teaspoonful of chives finely cut. Melt 2 oz of butter and mix all together.

Put the stuffing in lightly, leaving room for the oatmeal to swell. Sew the herring up with needle and thread and bake them in a greased baking tin in a moderate oven for 40 minutes, basting them from time to time.

Red Herring: The Old Boy's Way

Choose plump fish without melts or roe, and remove the head and tail. Split the fish open down the front and place them on the brander over a pan. Cover them with whisky some of which will spill over into the tin. Light the whisky, above and below, and when the flame dies down, eat them with the fingers.

Red Herring with Beer

Top, tail and split open the fish, lay them on an ashet and cover them with warm beer. Leave them for about an hour, drain well and brander over a clear fire.

Oysters

There are many ways in which the cook can use oysters but the gourmet admits to one only—eating them the minute the shells are opened. Quarters of lemon and brown bread and butter go well with them.

For the fastidious who have qualms about eating them raw, it is well to remember that the opening of the shell kills the mollusc instantly.

Dressing a Partan (Crab)

Crabs are easy to buy cooked but if you have an uncooked crab boil it for 20 to 30 minutes. When it is quite cold wipe it well with a damp cloth and then put it on its back, its tail towards you. Remove all claws by twisting inwards and towards you. Put your thumbs under the flap, push up and the break the body away from the shell.

With the mouth of the shell facing you, and again using your thumbs, press down and forwards and the stomach bag with mouth attached will come away with a click. Discard this. If there are eggs, discard them also. Remove all the soft brown meat from the shell and put it in a bowl.

There is a false line around the shell cavity, tap sharply round it and the edges will break easily. Wash the shell, dry it and rub it lightly with salad oil. Take the body of the crab and remove the lungs (known as 'Dead men's fingers') which are an ugly greenish colour. There will be some more brown meat, which should be added to the meat in the bowl. Scoop out the meat from the leg sockets and add it. Break the claws and remove the white meat.

Mash the brown meat, add a tablespoonful of soft white breadcrumbs, season to taste with pepper, salt and a little salad cream. Pile into either end of the shell. Shred the white meat, season it lightly and fill it into the centre of the shell. Hardboiled egg put through a sieve makes an attractive finish.

Tomato salad, cucumber and lettuce are ideal to serve with dressed partan. Chopped parsley, grated nutmeg or a suspicion of grated mace also go well with crab meat. It is of the utmost importance that you do not spoil this dish with fragments of shell.

Lobster Morar

There comes a point when nothing can be gained and much lost in further cooking and never more so than in the cooking of shellfish; and subsequent dressing should not involve further cooking either. The cock lobster is held to be of much finer flavour than the hen but the hen is chosen in preference because of the coral or spawn.

For this dish it is advisable to choose a large hen lobster. Kill it by severing the spinal cord at the back of the head and then plunge it into a goblet of sea water quickly brought to boiling point. The blue-black shell will turn to the familiar lobster red. The cooking time must be judged by the size but 30 minutes should be sufficient unless the fish weighs 6 or 7 lb in which case 1 hour will be needed.

While the lobster is boiling, infuse an onion finely sliced, a saltspoonful of mustard, a saltspoonful of ground nutmeg, a small blade of mace, a teaspoonful of lemon zest and a teaspoonful of anchovy essence in a pint of water. Poach two large fillets of lemon sole without skin in a pint of cream, slightly salted.

When cool enough to handle remove all the white meat from the body and claws and place it in a bowl to keep warm but do not cook it. Lift the sole from the cream, break into pieces and add to the lobster meat. Strain the cream which should be down to about half a pint. Strain the infused stock which should also be down to about half a pint.

Bring 2 oz of butter in a saucepan to sizzling point and add 1½ oz of plain white flour, cook it in the butter for a little and then gradually add the stock. Cook for 5 minutes and then slowly add the cream and some of the coral. Add salt to taste and a dust of white pepper. Empty the sole and lobster on to a hot ashet, pour the sauce over it and top with the rest of the coral.

To do more to this dish is to gild the lily but a bed of the following forcemeat is quite acceptable. Boil two crabs in sea water for about 20 minutes. Shred all the white meat from the body and claws. Pour some of the liquor in which the crabs were cooked into a pan with an ounce or so of butter. Add the meat, and sufficient fine white breadcrumbs, slightly flavoured with salt and pepper, to make the mixture solid. Shell three hard-boiled eggs, slice them, and remove the yolks from the whites.

Make a bed of the forcemeat on a warm ashet and lay the whites of the eggs on this. Dish the lobster and sole in a mound on top of the eggs and cover with the sauce. Put the yolks through a fine sieve over the sauce and the remainder of the coral over them. (A much finer texture is obtained from egg yolk if it is put through a sieve while it is still warm, and the whites are more pleasant to eat if they are not allowed to get cold.)

Shrimps and Prawns

These, too, should be boiled in sharply boiling sea water: 6 minutes for shrimps and 8 for prawns. In some kitchens where they were much used, the iron, on which dilse was curled, was brought to red heat and plunged into the pan of boiling water to bring it back to the right temperature after the shellfish had been dropped into the water.

Both shrimps and prawns make a fine sauce to serve with fish dishes, anchovy being added more for colour than for flavour.

Fish Garnish

Savoury butter is simple and easy to make. Into, say 4 oz of butter, pound until absolutely smooth, one of the following ingredients— from which the butter obtains its name—parsley, blanched and finely chopped, curry, anchovy, crab, lobster, or shrimp.

Scallops

Scallops are a symbol of piety, an epicure's choice of shellfish, and a cat's frenzy. A cookery book is not the place to discuss the history of the scallop or the reason for the word 'piety'. It is sufficient to say that the scallop was the emblem of a religious order of pilgrims. Cat's Frenzy? When given a scallop a cat will, with dire threats in fierce cat-tongue, rush madly looking for a corner where it can devour this delicacy without even sharing the aroma. Incidently, I would not leave scallops unattended for a second if even the douciest cat were around.

There are two important points to remember when cooking scallops: they must not be over-cooked, and their flavour must not be smothered. Allow 12 scallops for 4 shells when serving. Free them: there is a large creamy body, a darkish yellow beard, and roe. Give the beards a 'chap' with the meat mallet and simmer them in $\frac{1}{2}$ a pint of water with pepper, salt, chopped parsley, a saltspoonful of curry powder and a sliver or two of onion for 30 minutes.

Scrub, rinse, dry and oil the shells. Melt a knob of butter in a saucepan, slice the flesh and toss it in the hot butter; but on no account brown it. Strain the liquor over them and cook gently for 15 minutes. Add just enough soft white breadcrumbs, slightly seasoned with a dust of salt and pepper, to thicken the liquor and no more. Put the mixture into the shells with the roe on top, dust lightly with breadcrumbs then dot with 'peas' of butter.

Bake in a hot oven just long enough for the top to become crisp. This is a fairly standard recipe. I personally prefer to make a liquor with the beards and seasoning as mentioned *but* without the parsley. I blanch a bunch of parsley, cool it and chop finely, then pound it into some butter. I make these into miniature balls, and 'bead' the top of the shells with it.

Scallops in Sauce

Make the liquor as instructed in the preceding recipe but omit the curry powder. Strain it and cook the scallops halved, and the roe cut into pieces, for 15 minutes in the liquor. Remove them from the liquor which should be made up to half a pint, add half a pint of cream and make a sauce in the usual way. Taste for seasoning. Add the meat, bring to the boil and no more.

Serve with snippets of toast to sup the sauce.

Fish Terrine

The making of a fish terrine is a most rewarding, even exciting, experience. The scope is endless as individual taste and the great variety of fish makes many combinations possible. This is a basic recipe for which you require both cooked and raw fish in fillets or strips, and a casserole or terrine with a close-fitting lid.

1 lb cooked weight of fish without skin or bone	1 teaspoonful finely grated lemon rind
Fresh fillets	Salt, pepper, and a dust of paprika
2 tablespoonfuls celery	
2 tablespoonfuls onion	White wine
2 tablespoonfuls cream	Melted butter with a little pepper and salt in it
2 eggs, well beaten	
1 teaspoonful finely chopped parsley	Butter (to butter the terrine or casserole heavily)

Parboil the celery and the onion for a few minutes to mellow the flavour and chop them finely. Put the cooked fish into a roomy bowl and pound it until smooth; then begin to work in all the other ingredients except the fillets, the wine, and the seasoned butter. Taste and season further if necessary. Make sure the fillets are quite dry and butter them with the seasoned melted butter.

Now build up the terrine by laying a foundation base of the forcemeat in the well-buttered dish, keeping it just clear of the sides of the dish. Put a layer of fish over it, then more forcemeat, then more fillets until all the ingredients are used, the last layer being fillets. There should be just the merest space between the dish and the filling, enough to let you run a fine spatula round the inside.

Spoon the wine over the dish, filling it down the sides. Cook in a moderate oven for 1 hour with a close-fitting lid on the dish.

Note: This dish should not brown or crisp: the wine helps to prevent this. Some cooks like to cook a terrine set in a pan of gently boiling water in the oven.

When quite cold turn the terrine carefully out on a bed of very crisp lettuce in a suitable dish. Coat with aspic jelly or mayonnaise aspic, and decorate with shrimps, prawns, slivers of lemon, crisp parsley, or even cooked fish roe.

A Salmon Terrine

Use the above method without onion and wine, *but* with some diced peeled cucumber, and a cup of cucumber juice for spooning over the dish.

Salmon Paté

With some good fish trimmings make a stock flavoured with white peppercorns, a piece of onion, a spray of parsley, three allspice, a blade of mace, a little salt and some crushed basil. Strain into a flattish pan and add some slices of salmon. Bring to the boil and cook gently but well. Let it cool in the liquor.

If there is skin or bone remove it and weigh the fish. Pound the fish in the mortar until very smooth. Now add melted butter to the proportion of 2 oz to the pound of fish and more salt if necessary.

Pack very firmly into little pots, taking great care that there are no air pockets, and cover with clarified butter. Ensure a perfect seal with the rim of the pot.

Soused Herring

Use boned herring dried on a towel for this recipe. Dust well with pepper and salt and roll them up tightly, skin side out. Place them firmly in a pie-dish or a casserole and cover with vinegar and water in equal quantities. Add a piece of mace, a few peppercorns and cloves and bake in a moderate oven until firm and brown (about 45 minutes).

Soused Herring (Without Vinegar)

This is an old Scots method, in which the herrings are washed, trimmed and boned. Sprinkle them with salt and pepper, roll them up tightly and pack them into a buttered pie-dish. Cover with sour milk and cook in a moderate oven for 30 minutes after the milk comes to the boil. This gives a perfect flavour.

Serve with lettuce.

Soused Trout

Clean and bone smallish trout and treat as for herring with equal quantities of vinegar and water.

Tatties-n-herrin': Salt Herring

Salt herring must be mellowed by soaking in cold water for 24 hours and the water should be changed twice in that time. They can also be mellowed by soaking in skimmed milk. After mellowing, rub off any scales that may be left and head-and-tail the fish.

Wash the required number of potatoes (which are better for this dish if left in their jackets) and make a sharp incision down the side of each potato. Place the potatoes in a roomy pot, add cold water, not quite covering them: but do not add salt.

Place the required number of herring, mellowed and cleaned, evenly on top of the potatoes. Put the lid on and boil gently until the potatoes are cooked by which time the herring will also be cooked. Lift the fish on to a hot ashet, pour the potatoes, and shake them well. Let them steam for 5 minutes.

Serve butter with this dish.

Kedgeree

1 lb cooked fish free from all skin and bone	2 eggs and 1 oz butter
4 oz whole rice	Pepper, salt and a dessertspoonful of chopped parsley

You can cook fish specially for this, but it is a good way of using up cold, left-over fish. Boil the rice in plenty of water slightly salted. Cook it until each grain is tender (but not mushy) and strain it.

While the rice is cooking, hard boil the eggs, shell them and chop them up finely while still warm. Melt the butter in a saucepan, toss the fish in it until it is hot, then add the rice, the chopped egg and the parsley. Mix well adding some pepper and serve very hot.

Note: A cup of cream can be used instead of the butter.

Liver Haggis in a Cod's Head

2 cods' livers	Pepper and salt
1 large onion	1 cod's head
½ lb oatmeal	

Wash the head thoroughly in cold salted water. Parboil the onion and chop it into little pieces. Remove any strings in the livers and beat them with a fork. Put the oatmeal into a mixing bowl, add the onion, pepper and salt and the creamed livers.

Mix well and then stuff the cod's head with the mixture. Butter some strong greaseproof paper and tie the head securely in it; then tie the bundle in a pudding cloth. Steam or boil for 1½ hours.

Salmon

The perfect way to cook a whole salmon is in water just under the boil (a form of poaching). Clean the fish but handle it as little as possible. Leave on the head, tail and scales. Have the fish kettle ready with enough water to cover the fish. Add a tablespoonful of salt,* a saltspoonful of bicarbonate of soda and bring the water to the boil.

Cook the fish in the boiling water for 5 minutes, then reduce the temperature by adding a teacupful of cold water and drawing the kettle away from direct heat. Let it remain so, just under boiling point until it is cooked. Remove the kettle from the heat altogether and leave it for 15 minutes.

Time required for cooking—Grilse (about 8 lb) 30 minutes
Salmon (6 lb, fairly thick) 45 min.; A 1 lb slice 15 min.

*Salt: 1 tablespoonful to a gallon of water.

Hairy Tatties

Hairy tatties are made with dry salted cod which you can buy in small pieces. Soak the cod in salt water for 24 hours, changing the water twice.

Use just enough cold water to cover it, bring it to the boil and cook for 30 minutes. Cool the fish, skin and bone it and break up into little flakes. Take a fork or a wire beater and beat the flakes into a pot of well mashed potatoes. Add a lump of butter, some black pepper and beat well. Do not salt the potatoes in case the fish is still very salty.

The flakes break up as fine as hairs, hence the name. The dish is now ready to eat but you can put it into a buttered pie-dish and bake it in a moderate oven, dotting the top with knobs of butter.

Fish Patties

The secret of a tasty patty is in its smoothness. Take equal quantities of cooked fish and cooked potatoes. Flake the fish, break it down as fine as you can and mash the potatoes very smooth.

Drop a knob of butter into a pan, add the fish and then the potatoes, add salt and pepper if necessary, and cook the mixture a little, stirring well.

Let it cool then add one well beaten egg, mix well and shape into patties. Dip them in beaten egg and then roll them in breadcrumbs. Fry in fat just at smoking hot point until they are brown and crisp. Drain well on kitchen paper.

Fish Pie with Salt Fish

In the making up of this pie add no salt except in the sauce. Mellow the fish for 24 hours in either skimmed milk, buttermilk or water, then cook until tender. Boil the required number of potatoes: slice half of them and mash the other half adding a little black pepper. Make a really good sauce with plenty of mustard until it 'bites'. Now assemble your pie.

Assemble the pie by greasing a roomy pie-dish with a liberal coating of butter. Put in a layer of sliced potato, then a layer of fish and then a layer of sauce. Repeat until you have used all the sliced potato, fish and sauce. Make the final covering with mashed potatoes, pour melted butter over it and bake until the mixture comes to the boil and the top is nicely browned.

(I met this pie on the West Coast of Scotland and the lady of the house had a large silver thimble with which she made dints in the top of the pie and then filled them with melted butter).

Salt Fish with a Cheese Sauce

2 lb salt fish
2 oz butter
1½ oz flour
1 pint milk

Pepper, a teaspoonful mustard
(no salt)
4 oz grated cheese

Soak the salt fish in milk or water or a mixture of milk and water for 24 hours, changing the liquid twice in that time. Put the fish in cold water, bring it to the boil and cook slowly until it flakes easily.

Make the white sauce by heating the butter in a saucepan: mix in the flour, cook it a little, then slowly add the milk. Stir steadily until the sauce is smooth and boil it for 5 minutes, stirring all the time. Blend the mustard in a little water, add it, and then mix in the cheese. Remove the skin and bone from the fish, flake it and put it into the sauce.

A mealy dumpling is often served with this dish together with mashed potatoes.

Tinker's Trout

Take any number of trout, of an even size, wash them, trim off the head and tail, and clean them out without cutting up the belly skin. Boil for 5 minutes in some of the water in which they were caught, well salted.

Lift them out of the water, drain on a towel or a brander, fill in the belly with chopped watercress and butter and grill over a clear fire.

Sea Trout: Colin Livet's Recipe

If the trout are small wash them, take off the head and tail, and gut them. Dust well with salt all over and leave for 2 hours. Dip them in milk, let them drip and then coat them well with very fine oatmeal. Fry gently in olive oil, and do not let them get very brown. Cook until the fish comes away from the back bone when tried with a fork.

Add some chopped chives to the oil, a gill of hot water, season with wine vinegar, and boil up; give a shake of pepper and serve in a tureen with the fish.

If the fish are large, fillet them and cook in the same way.

Beef, Game, Mutton and Pork

Meat

A sirloin of beef is perhaps the best for roasting but a rib roast makes very fine eating. A fillet of beef can also be treated as a joint and roasted; it needs much basting and does not take long to cook.

In choosing a joint allow 6 oz of beef per person. It must not be very fat, on the other hand it should not be too lean as lean beef can be tough. Immediately it comes from the shop remove the paper wrapping as paper can be greedy with beef juice. If the joint is to be kept for some time, even a few hours, do not hang it with the cut surface down else it will drip.

When the roast is in the oven on no account stab it with a fork or skewer as the juices will rush out behind the prongs. If it must be skewered, do so before it goes into the oven and leave the skewer in place until just before putting the meat on the table.

Beef Olives

1 lb thinly cut stewing steak	4 to 6 olives, stoned and
1 cupful soft white bread-	chopped fine
crumbs	Pepper and salt
1 large onion minced	1 oz butter
	2 tablespoonfuls warm water

Cut the steak into strips about 3 inches long and 2 inches wide. Give it a gentle beat to make it tender. Mix the breadcrumbs, onion, olives and pepper and salt in a bowl; melt the butter in the water and mix to a soft paste. Put a tight little roll of stuffing on each piece of steak and roll up the meat. Tie firmly with fine twine.

Heat some dripping in the stewpan. Brown the olives and then lift them out of the pan. If there is a lot of fat take most of it out of the pan, then stir in some flour and let it cook a little. Add stock or water and bring to the boil. Season a little with pepper and salt, then lay the olives in the pan, and bring to the boil again.

Let them cook gently, hardly more than simmering, for 1½ hours. Try the meat and give it a little longer if necessary. Add browning if necessary.

Boiled Beef and Suet Dumplings

If you are not sure how to choose a cut of beef for boiling, be guided by your butcher, but make sure that there is not a large proportion of bone and fat. Allow 4 to 6 oz per person.

In a roomy pan use enough water to cover the meat and some pieces of carrot and turnip and an onion. Put the meat into boiling water, leave the pan on full heat until it comes to the boil again and then lower the heat and let the meat cook gently. Skim the stock from time to time.

The cooking time must be ruled by the size of the cut and the age of the animal from which it was cut. However, it will not be ready under $2\frac{1}{2}$ hours (it may take 3 hours). The vegetables will cook in $1\frac{1}{2}$ hours and the dumplings in 15 minutes.

Season with pepper and salt.

Suet Dumplings

8 oz plain flour   1 teaspoonful baking powder
2 oz shredded suet $\frac{1}{2}$ teaspoonful salt

This quantity will make six to eight dumplings.

Rub the suet into the flour, add the baking powder and the salt and mix to a stiff dough with cold water. Flour the hands well and make the dough into the required number of balls.

Drop them into the boiling stock 15 minutes before mealtime. If there is not enough room for them, dish the meat and vegetables, keeping them hot while the dumplings cook.

Beefsteak and Kidney Pudding

Crust
- $\frac{1}{2}$ lb flour
- $\frac{1}{4}$ lb finely shredded suet
- $\frac{1}{2}$ teaspoonful baking powder
- Saltspoonful of salt
- Cold water

Filling
- 1 lb lean beef
- 2 mutton kidneys
- Pepper and salt
- A dessertspoonful of chopped onion
- $\frac{1}{2}$ lb button mushrooms, sliced

To make the crust rub the suet into the flour, add the salt and baking powder and mix to a firm dough with a little cold water. Divide into two pieces, one to line a pudding bowl and the other to make a lid. Roll out the larger piece and line the well-greased pudding bowl. Roll out the second piece, keeping it round and big enough to fit neatly on to the bowl.

Cut the beef and the kidneys into small pieces, removing the core of fat and the skin from the kidneys. Dust freely with flour mixed with pepper and salt. Place the meat in the bowl along with the onion and mushrooms. Add a cupful of cold water.

Moisten the lid with cold water and fit it neatly on, pressing the edges well together. Then tie on a pudding cloth securely.

Put the bowl into a pan of boiling water with enough water to cover it entirely and let the pudding boil for 3 hours.

Roasting a Joint

Weigh the joint, wipe it with a damp towel, and put it into a roasting tin in which there is a little hot fat. Place it in a very hot preheated oven and after 15 minutes turn down the heat and let the joint cook gently for the required time. If the heat is right it should keep up a gentle spluttering protest (if there is no sound the oven is not hot enough). Baste frequently—every 15 minutes if possible. Time for roasting: 15 minutes to every pound of beef and 15 minutes over.

If you intend to have roast potatoes with the beef, parboil them for 5 minutes, shake very dry and arrange them around the joint. Time them to be ready at the same time as the meat.

Gravy

Put the joint on a hot ashet. If there are potatoes, lift them into a hot vegetable dish. Strain the fat off into a bowl, taking great care to retain the brown meat juice. Pour in a pint of boiling water, add pepper and salt and bring through the boil.

Mince Collops (1)

The old Scots method of making mince collops was to mince or cut very finely some tender beef with a sharp knife. To this was added a spoonful of really good suet, chopped very small and with all skin removed, some chopped onion or chives and black pepper and salt.

This was lightly fried in a pan, some flour dusted over it, a little hot water added and the mince was ready.

Mince Collops (2)

To a quantity of minced or very finely chopped beef steak add a spoonful of finely chopped suet, some chopped onion, black pepper and salt.

Form into patties and brander over a clear fire until crisp and brown. Time: about 15 minutes. (Instead of using a brander the patties can be fried or grilled).

Mince Collops with Dumplings

Make the mince as in the following recipe but use a pint of water. If this boils away, see that it is made up before the dumplings are put in as a lot of gravy is essential.

Dumplings

2 oz plain white flour
1 oz fine oatmeal
1½ oz finely shredded suet
A spoonful of grated onion

Pepper, salt and a small level teaspoonful of baking powder
Cold water

Mix all the ingredients together and add just enough water to make a stiff dough. Flour your hands and make the dough into small balls and arrange on top of the mince.

They will be light and fully cooked in just 15 minutes so do not cook them any longer. Time their entry into the pan just 15 minutes before they are to be eaten.

Mince Steak with Rice and Poached Eggs

1 lb minced steak
1 oz flour
1 oz dripping or butter

1 onion, finely chopped
Pepper and salt
½ pint hot water

Melt the butter or dripping in a stewpan and fry the onion lightly in it. Then add the mince and brown it, stirring until all the pieces are separate and brown. Season with pepper and salt and dust in the flour. Then add the hot water and bring to the boil. Cook gently until the meat is tender: this will take about an hour.

Boil 6 oz of whole rice quickly in boiling salted water until tender. Drain well. Poach one egg per person.

Dish the mince on a hot ashet, arrange the rice round it and put the well drained poached eggs in the centre of the dish.

Minced Beef Pudding

Paste

½ lb plain white flour
6 oz grated raw potato
4 oz butter

1 teaspoonful baking powder
½ teaspoonful salt
A good shake of black pepper

Rub the butter into the flour, add the baking powder, the salt and pepper and then the raw potato. Add a little water to make a dough: very little is needed as the potato makes it very moist. Knead the dough and cut it into five pieces. Grease a pudding basin.

Season 1 lb of raw minced beef with pepper, salt and a tablespoonful of finely chopped blanched onion. Add 2 tablespoonfuls of water and mix well. Divide into four equal portions.

Roll out a piece of paste to cover the bottom of the basin and spread one portion of mince on it, leaving a little margin clear. Cover with another layer of paste, pinching the edges to make them meet. Continue until all the portions are used up.

Finish with a lid of paste. Cover with greased paper and tie on a pudding cloth tightly. Steam steadily for 3 hours. (This can also make a good meat roly-poly.)

Roast Fillet of Beef

Try to obtain a piece of fillet of equal thickness; if it trails off in a thin tail this must be cut off as it would merely dry up before the thick part is cooked. Do not trim off any fat. Put it into a hot oven in a roasting tin with some hot dripping, turn down the heat after 15 minutes and let it cook gently, basting it from time to time. Time: 15 minutes to the pound.

Grilled Fillet Steak

Cut the required number of steaks from a fillet of beef. Beat them with a cutlet bat and season with pepper and salt. Brush freely with melted butter; heat the gridiron and rub it with suet. Arrange the slices on it and brown quickly under the grill: turn and brown on the other side. Lower the heat a little and finish cooking, turning the slices occasionally. Time: 8 minutes to each side.

To serve, arrange on a hot dish and pour the juices, which have dripped into the pan, over them. Grilled mushrooms and grilled tomatoes are the ideal accompaniment, together with crisp potato chips.

Liver and Bacon Casserole

1 lb liver, sliced	4 oz soft white breadcrumbs
4 oz bacon rashers	Pepper, salt and a saltspoonful
4 oz onion	mustard
4 oz mushrooms	Butter or dripping, or ham fat
4 oz cooking apple	

Cut the liver into individual pieces and trim the rind off the bacon. Parboil the onion and cut it in four; peel the apple and quarter it also; peel the mushrooms. Heat the fat—preferably ham fat—in a stewpan. Lightly fry the bacon and liver. Take a casserole and put in all the ingredients well-mixed and pour in a cupful of stock or hot water.

Season the breadcrumbs with the pepper, salt and mustard and spread lightly over the top of the contents of the casserole; then moisten them with some of the fat in which the liver and bacon were fried. Cook for 1 hour in a moderate oven.

The top should be brown and crisp when brought to the table.

Steak and Kidney Pie

It used to be considered correct to use puff pastry to cover a pie but flaky paste or short crust are equally good.

There are two ways of cooking a pie: one by covering meat that is already partly cooked, and the other by cooking meat and paste together. Many believe that cooking the meat and the paste together from scratch makes the perfect pie, but if you cover meat already half cooked you avoid a lot of heartburning about the pastry being overcooked long before the meat is ready.

The Filling

    1 lb steak
    ½ lb ox kidney *or* 3 mutton kidneys

Cut the steak into small pieces, removing any unnecessary fat, and season with pepper and salt and a good dusting of flour. Cut the kidney into small pieces and remove any fatty core. Season and dust with flour. Put into a casserole, add half a cupful of water or stock and some slices of onion; put the lid on and cook in a moderate oven for 1 hour.

When arranging it in the pie-dish, do not add the onion. Add more stock if you think it necessary—even a little browning can be an improvement.

Puff Paste

Sift 8 oz of flour and a good pinch of salt into a very cold basin. Make a well in the centre and pour in a little cold water to which you have added a teaspoonful of lemon juice. This should make a very firm dough. Turn it out on to a floured board or a marble slab and knead it lightly using as little flour as possible. When the dough is quite smooth and pliable roll it out in a long narrow strip, keeping the corners square.

Wash 6 oz of butter in cold water, dry it on a clean towel or a piece of muslin, and work it until it becomes as pliable as the dough but do not make it too soft. Shape it into a thin flat cake. The paste should be just a little wider than the size of the pat of butter, and twice as long. Put the butter at one end of the paste and bring the other end over to cover it; pinch the ends to seal. Give the paste a half turn to the right. This brings the open end towards you and from you. Dust a little flour over and under the paste, and with quick, short forward strokes roll it out in a long strip.

Keep the paste an even thickness, fold it in three and give it a half turn to bring the ends to and from you and roll it out again. Fold again in three and set aside for 30 minutes. Cover it with a towel and keep very cool. In all it should have seven rollings with a rest between every two. The longer it rests the better it will be when cooked.

For the last rolling, rool out the paste a little wider than the dish it is to cover. Cut a narrow band from the edge, brush the edge of the pie-dish with cold water and fit the strip lightly and evenly. Do not press it down as this will bruise the 'leaves'. Cut another band, a little wider this time.

Now fill in the meat, add the gravy and brush the band of paste on the dish. Lay on the cover of paste. Take the pie-dish in the left hand and with a sharp knife trim round the edge, holding the knife away from you so that the handle slopes in towards the dish. (Do not trim it too much as the paste will shrink a little.) Flake up the edges with the back of the knife and mark the edge in spaces of about 7 inches, holding the knife vertically. Cut the remaining strip into diamond shapes to form leaves. Mark them too, making vein marks with the point of the knife. Make a sharp cut in the centre of the pie cover, wet the leaves and arrange them in the centre around the cut, but not covering it.

Brush the top of the paste with well beaten egg, taking care that it does not run down the sides. (If you allow it to run down the sides it will seal the paste and it will not rise evenly.)

Cook in a hot oven for 15 minutes then reduce the heat and bring the pie to boiling point. Cook for at least 30 minutes after the meat has come to the boil. Add more gravy just before serving, if necessary.

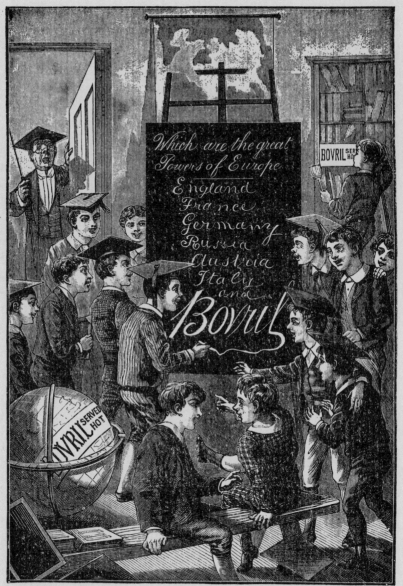

THE 1000 GUINEAS CHALLENGE.

Potted Ox Cheek

The old Scots recipes called for ox heads and cow heels, but a delectable potted head can be made with two ox cheeks and a knap bone washed well in salted water and then placed in a roomy pot with a gallon of water and a tablespoonful of salt.

Bring slowly to the boil, skimming well: keep on skimming for about 15 minutes after it comes to the boil. Add a dozen peppercorns and let it cook slowly until the meat is tender. This will take 3 hours or even a little longer.

When the meat is quite cooked, lift out the bone and the cheeks and strain the stock into a bowl. Let it sit overnight so that it will be possible to lift off the fat cleanly. The stock will have boiled in and, between skimming and boiling in, it should be down to 4 pints. Go over the meat carefully, skin the palate, remove all fat and any pieces of membrane, and mince the rest. Give it a good shake of black pepper.

Next day return it to the pot with the stock. Taste for salt and pepper and bring slowly to the boil, skimming all the time. (Skimming is the secret of a clear, sweet potted head.) Bring through the boil and let it boil gently for 15 minutes. Allow it to cool a little, then lift it into bowls.

Pigeon Pie

4 pigeons	An onion
1 lb lean steak	Pepper, salt, a blade of mace
A few slices of fat bacon	and three cloves
A bunch of parsley	Pie paste

Pluck, clean and cut off the feet of the birds. Scald the feet and lay them aside. Cut the steak into small pieces. Roll up the bacon with the mace inside. Stick the cloves into the onion. Divide the birds into quarters.

Put some flour on a plate, season it well with pepper and salt and roll the portions of bird and the steak in it, coating them as liberally as possible.

Place all the ingredients in a casserole or any fireproof dish with a lid and just cover them with warm water. Replace the lid and put the dish in a moderate oven. Let it cook until the birds are tender: this depends on the age of the birds, but it may take 1½ hours. Keep up the level of gravy with boiling water.

When cooked, let it cool before removing the bacon, parsley and the onion, all of which are now too highly flavoured to be palatable. Add more salt and pepper if necessary.

Cover with a good pie pastry, leaving a wide hole in the centre. Brush heavily with beaten egg and bake in a hot oven until the pastry is risen; then lower the heat a little and leave until the pastry is cooked. Add more gravy if necessary.

Glaze the feet and just before putting the dish on the table, put them in the centre of the pie as if the birds were coming out feet first. Cut off claws.

Liver Pudding : Colonel Cameron's Recipe

1 lb liver and some fatty bacon	Salt, pepper and a salt spoon-
1 large firm onion	ful of ground mace
4 oz fine breadcrumbs	2 eggs
4 oz fine oatmeal	

Parboil a piece of liver (calf's if possible); then remove all skin and any vein. Grate or chop finely. Cut up the bacon into pieces which should not be too thin. Parboil a large firm onion or a few small ones and chop them.

Mix the liver, bacon and onion together and add the bread-crumbs, the oatmeal and the seasoning. Beat the eggs until they are frothy and, with some liquor from the pan in which the liver was parboiled, bind the mixture to a good firmness.

Flour the hands well and shape the mixture into a roll. Take a strong firm pudding cloth, scald it, wring it out and flour it well. Put the pudding into it, tie it up firmly (but not too tightly) and boil it in a pan of water with a plate in the bottom for 3 hours.

Pan Pie

Use the same ingredients and quantities as for steak and kidney pudding and prepare them in the same way. Heat a little good dripping in a stew pan and lightly fry the onion in it; then lift it out and brown the steak and kidney. Replace the onion, add a little hot water and let the meat cook gently for 1 hour.

Make the paste and roll it out on a well-floured board, keeping it in the round and slightly smaller than the pan. Add a cupful of warm water or gravy to the stew and taste for seasoning: add more if necessary then lay the paste on top. Put the lid on the pan and let the pie cook gently for 1 hour. (Do not lift the lid unless it is absolutely necessary.)

To serve, cut the round of paste in eight triangles and arrange them on a hot ashet. Pile the steak and kidney on top.

Venison

Venison may be red deer (stag or hind) or fallow deer (buck or doe) or even roe deer but the treatment is almost the same in each case. Venison is almost always very lean and to be tender must be well hung (your butcher will not have it on his counter until it is ready for cooking). It is good roasted, braised, or pot roasted, and fried steaks are *par excellence*—but they are for the expert. The 'big house' method of roasting a haunch was to make a 'hap' of flour and water, and perhaps a little dripping, into a hard paste which could withstand long cooking. I do not think this method can be bettered even with a small cut.

Venison and hare are both much improved by lying in a marinade for 24 hours. Two sisters, daughters of a Perthshire laird, had very sound ideas on the cooking of game and they often agreed to differ.

Miss Matty's Marinade

Miss Matty believed that the finest marinade was made with a bottle of white wine, half as much salad oil and a cup of onion juice all beaten together.

Miss Maggie's Marinade

The quantities depend on the amount of meat to be covered but the basic recipe is:

6 tablespoonfuls olive oil	Some bay leaves crushed
2 tablespoonfuls wine vinegar	Pepper and a little ground
A cupful finely chopped parsley	clove
A cupful of crushed herbs, rosemary, savoury and thyme	Enough sliced onions to cover the meat completely

Less sophisticated recipes give vinegar and oil as a marinade, in which case I would dilute the vinegar with an equal quantity of water. Portions of meat which have been soaking in a marinade should be drained dry and even patted lightly in a clean towel and then dusted with flour. As a start to cooking them, they should be lightly fried in butter or roast fat just enough to 'set' the meat. The marinade is usually added and when it is mixed with crushed herbs should be strained before going into the cooking pot.

Jugged Venison

Cut the required amount of venison into cubes, slightly smaller than the size of an egg. Cut a thickish piece of not too lean bacon (a little less than half the amount of venison) in the same way.

Heat some bacon fat in the dish in which you are to cook the jug: this should be earthenware if possible, but a pot or casserole with a very close fitting lid is adequate. Add the bacon chunks and fry them, stirring them about well until they are set. Remove them and do the same with the venison. Take it out, brown slightly a handful of shallots and remove them also. If most of the fat is used up by this time add some more, and put in what you judge to be enough flour to thicken your dish. Cook it, then add stock and claret in the ratio of a quart of good stock to a pint of claret.

Season with pepper, salt, a pinch of ground mace and ground clove, plenty of black pepper and bring to the boil. Put in the venison, the bacon and the shallots and cover the pot closely. Cook for at least 2½ hours, making sure that it does not boil in (but avoid lifting the lid frequently). Fry a bowlful of button mushrooms in butter and drop them in 30 minutes before dishing the jug.

Season to taste before taking to the table.

Colonel Cameron's Roast Haunch of Venison

Choose buck venison with dark meat and a good depth of clear white fat. Tie it in fine muslin and hang for at least a fortnight in a cool larder during which time it should be examined frequently and wiped with a dry cloth if necessary.

When ready for use, wipe it all over carefully with a dry cloth and wrap it in thickly buttered paper. Then make a paste with flour and enough water to mix it to a stiff workable mixture. Cover the haunch with this and cover again with buttered paper, tying it on securely.

Roast before a clear fire, keeping the heat up, allowing 20 minutes per pound of venison. Twenty minutes before you judge it to be ready, take off the paper and paste carefully, catching the juice therein. Return the joint to the fire and baste carefully with butter until it is brown all over.

It is just as good baked in an oven in which case it should be set in all its coats on a brander or spars but not in a tin.

5*

Miss Maggie's Venison Pasty

Cut a portion of venison, about a pound or a little more, into tiny pieces. Cook them long and slowly in butter and season well with pepper and salt. Thicken the buttery liquid with a tablespoonful of flour and a very little water; cook for a few minutes then remove the pan from the fire. Pour in all the port wine it will take without making it runny, and let it cool.

Make a good puff paste and cut it into two equal squares. Spread the venison on one half and wet round the edges. Place the other half on top and press firmly round the edges taking great care not to ruin the layers of paste.

Bake in a moderately hot oven until the paste is cooked, pale brown and well risen.

Happit Venison

Venison having no fat can easily become very dry in cooking. Modern methods, such as a self-basting roaster and tin foil, are a great help but the old Scots method of 'happing' the joint or cut in a hard paste before cooking has never been excelled.

Choose a cut with very little bone in it, brush heavily with melted butter well seasoned with salt and black pepper. For the 'hap' rub 2 oz of butter or good dripping or even lard into $\frac{1}{2}$ lb of flour and make a very firm dough with a little cold water. Roll it out to a thickness of about $\frac{1}{4}$ inch, brush round the edges with cold water, put the joint on one half and 'hap' over the other piece so that the venison is quite covered. Do not pull or stretch the paste as it would burst in cooking, and make very sure that the edges are sealed.

Cook in a canny heat for 20 minutes to every pound of venison and another 20 minutes for good measure.

Highland Venison Patties

½ lb cooked venison	½ pint venison gravy
¼ lb oatmeal	Pepper and salt and a little
Tablespoonful of good dripping	celery salt
1 large onion	A pinch of ground mace

Mince or chop the venison; slice and chop the onion; put the dripping into a saucepan and lightly fry the onion. Then add the gravy and bring to the boil. Stir in the oatmeal, add the venison and the seasoning and cook gently for 15 minutes.

Pour out on a plate and let it cool. Shape into patties and fry in fat until brown.

Forcemeat (for Venison)

½ lb calf's liver	½ lb bacon

Fry the liver and bacon with a tiny piece of garlic in butter and add enough stock to cook. Put it through a sieve and season with pepper, salt, and a little cayenne.

Capercailzie: the family recipe

Although the 'caper', known as the turkey of the pine woods, is not a true native of Scotland, it is well known in some parts of the country, and was quite often on our table in my childhood. Cranberry jam from the local berries was made to serve with it.

Pluck, draw and wash the bird well and mop it with a dampish towel. Use a stuffing of equal quantities of oatmeal, suet chopped fine and shredded onion, and pepper and salt to fill the body cavity. Sew up the bird, pin back the legs and wings; brown well in melted suet in a large iron pot. Take the bird out and brown a bowlful of sliced onions. Stir in a handful or so of flour, and then add some warm water, pepper and salt.

Replace the onions, lay the bird on top, dust it with pepper and salt and grated mace, then put the lid on the pot and cook the bird long and slowly until tender. Hare stock was sometimes added, and raw hare bones were even put round the bird in cooking. The legs were excellent devilled.

Braised Capercailzie with Cranberry Jelly

This recipe was used in the Clova House, Lumsden, kitchens in Victorian times when the 'caper' was breeding well in that area. A huge oval cast iron pot, the same shape as a fish kettle, was used. The bird's body cavity was stuffed with breadcrumbs, parsley, suet, chopped shallots, and pepper and salt; cranberries, when in season, were used with a little brown sugar. And the crop was stuffed with a veal forcemeat stuffing.

The bird was securely sewn, its legs and wings pinioned, and lowered into the pot almost full of boiling water, where it cooked for 15 minutes. It was then lifted out carefully, the pot emptied and a good lump of roast fat brought to boiling point in it.

The 'caper' was returned to the pot, the boiling fat spooned over it until the flesh crispened and the lid put on. The bird was then cooked slowly until quite tender (a 'caper' must be cooked to the very bone). The gravy was thickened with a pint of cranberry jelly and served in a separate tureen.

Celery or Brussels sprouts are ideal vegetables to serve with capercailzie.

Meaty Pancakes

4 oz plain white flour
1½ gills milk
1 egg
Pepper and salt

Teaspoonful of finely chopped onion
Teaspoonful of chopped parsley
Dripping or lard
4 oz cold cooked meat, minced

Make a batter with the flour, milk and egg. Mix until smooth and then beat well for at least 5 minutes. Mix the minced meat with the onion, parsley, pepper and salt. Add this to the batter. Melt a spoonful of lard or dripping in a frying pan and heat to a faint blue smoke.

Put in enough batter to cover the bottom of the pan and fry until golden brown. Turn the pancake over and brown the other side. Turn it out on to an ashet covered with greaseproof paper, fold it over and keep in a warm place; go on frying until all the mixture is used up.

The pancakes must be served soon after frying.

Happit Hen

1 boiling fowl
Carrot, turnip and onion
5 oz whole rice

A blade of mace
Salt

Sauce

2 oz butter
2 oz flour
1 gill chicken stock

1 gill milk or cream
1 egg
Pepper and salt

This is an old Scots method of serving a tough old bird.

Pluck, clean and truss the fowl and put it in a roomy pot with enough water to cover it. Let it cook long and slowly—it may take as long as 4 hours. Add carrot, turnip and onion but take them out when cooked. Season well with pepper and salt.

When the bird is tender, take the meat from the bones, remove all fat and gristle and cut into small portions. Strain the stock through a piece of linen to catch all the grease. Keep the meat hot in a spoonful of the stock along with carrot and turnip.

Cook the whole rice in a pint of stock until it is swollen, but not into a pudding. If you like mace, boil a blade along with the rice which can also be coloured with a few shreds of saffron. As the stock is well seasoned, it may not be necessary to add more seasoning, but avoid making the rice mushy by unnecessary stirring.

To make the sauce, heat the butter in a saucepan until it sizzles a little but do not brown it. Add the flour to it and stir until it is quite smooth, letting it cook a little. Add the liquid by degrees, season with pepper and salt, keeping in mind there is some seasoning in the chicken stock. Let the sauce cook for 5 minutes and meanwhile beat the egg in a warm, roomy bowl. Pour the boiling sauce over it, beating vigorously the while.

By this time you should have the rice arranged on a hot ashet in a bed with the pieces of fowl on top of it. Pour the hot sauce over and decorate with pieces of carrot and turnip.

Colonel Cameron's Meat Roll

1 lb lean beef	Pepper and salt
½ lb bacon	A saltspoonful of grated nutmeg
1 lb sausage meat	8 oz fine white breadcrumbs
3 hard-boiled eggs	A cupful of stock
2 eggs	

Mince the beef or chop it as fine as mince with a sharp knife, and do the same with the bacon. Mix the beef, bacon, sausage meat and breadcrumbs in a large mixing bowl, add the seasoning, the 2 eggs well beaten and then the stock. Work this until you have a perfectly smooth blend of all the ingredients.

Flour a board and spread the mixture out; put the hard-boiled eggs in it and roll it up, shaping it into a neat roll. Tie it up in a scalded pudding cloth, drop it into a pan of boiling water and cover it with a plate. Boil steadily for 2½ hours. Take it out of the pot, let it drip for a minute or two and then press it slightly between two ashets.

When it is quite cold, remove the cloth and glaze the roll.

Dressed Sheep's Head

For this the head is boiled whole. When quite tender lift it out of the broth and let it drip for some minutes before coating it thickly with brown breadcrumbs. Pour melted butter evenly over it and crisp it under a grill or over a hot fire.

Sheep's Head Pie

Remove the meat from cooked heads and cut away all veins and black parts. Skin the palate and the tongue; slice the tongue taking care to remove any small bones at the root. Remove the brains and put them in the bottom of the pie-dish.

Make half a pint of white sauce, add one tablespoonful of chopped parsley, two sliced hard-boiled eggs, and then the meat. Season to taste and mix well. Pour over the brains and then cover with a good pie crust. Bake in a moderate oven until the pastry is cooked. Since the meat in the pie is already cooked it needs no further cooking but it does enhance the flavour if the sauce comes to the boil.

Veal and Ham Pie

Use either flaky paste or rough puff paste for this pie and, as veal
is easily cooked, cook both the meat and the paste together.

1 lb veal	2 eggs
6 rashers bacon	Chopped parsley

Hard boil the eggs and cut them each into four quarters. If there
is rind on the bacon, cut it off and roll up the strips. Cut the veal
into small pieces. Mix well the veal, eggs, and bacon in a pie-dish,
and add a teaspoonful of chopped parsley. Add pepper, a very little
salt as the bacon may be salty, and stock.

Cover as for a steak pie and bake for 15 minutes in a hot oven;
then lower the heat and cook until the pastry is baked. Allow 1
hour's cooking time after the pie comes to the boil.

For stock, veal bones cooked for 45 minutes are useful.

This dish can be served hot or cold.

For the paste, sift $\frac{1}{2}$ lb of plain white flour into a basin and add
a pinch of salt. Cut 6 oz of shortening into small nobs and add to
the flour. Add 1 teaspoonful of lemon juice to 1 gill of cold water
and with this make the flour and shortening into a firm dough.
Knead lightly to make the paste smooth and roll it out in a strip
on a floured board. Fold the paste in three. Roll it out into a thin
strip again. Repeat the folding three times before rolling to the size
required to cover the dish, with a little over for decoration.

Note: RABBIT, FISH or CHICKEN PIE can be made in exactly
the same way, but with fish a white sauce should be used instead
of water or stock. Hard boiled eggs, parsley and a little grated
lemon rind go well with fish pie. Butter and lard in equal quantities
make the ideal shortening.

Pheasant

Given the choice I would roast a hen bird, the hen pheasant being much better eating than the showy cock bird. Pheasants should be well hung; in really cold weather this can be a week or ten days. The old test was to hang the bird by the tail and when the body fell down and left the tail behind it was ready for the pot.

Pluck carefully so that the skin is not torn, draw and wipe with a damp cloth. Roll a few shallots and a piece of butter, flour and black pepper into a ball about the size of a small egg, place it in the body cavity and truss the bird.

Cook it in a roasting tin in a fairly hot oven with some good fat —roast or bacon—and some strips of fat bacon over the bird. Reduce the heat after 15 minutes and allow the bird to cook at a gentle sizzle until tender. Remove the bacon and baste the bird until the skin bubbles and crinkles.

The cooking time depends on the age of the bird but overcooking should be avoided at all costs so that the moist, juicy flesh comes cleanly from the bone.

Keep the bird hot on a warm ashet. Remove some of the fat from the roasting tin and pour the gravy into a sauce tureen.

Serve with game chips or straw potatoes, a vegetable such as celery or tiny Brussels sprouts and a well seasoned bread sauce.

If fried breadcrumbs are served bread sauce is not necessary.

An old bird is excellent braised with wine and red currant jelly.

Partridge

Partridge is treated in exactly the same way as pheasant but butter only should be used to baste the bird. As the partridge is one of our finest game birds yet most delicate in flavour only the merest suspicion of flavouring should be used so that the taste of the bird is not lost.

Snipe and Woodcock

Snipe and woodcock may not feature often on a Scots menu as the woodcock in particular migrates just when he may be deemed ready for the table. Like all game they must be hung but not for more than two or three days, since they are served just as they are (except for the feathers) and the intestines, or trails, go off quickly.

For cooking, the birds are plucked from head to tail and singed, particular care being paid to the head. Remove the eyes and make the merest slit to take out the crop. The trails are considered a delicacy and the legs better than the breast. One mode of trussing is to fix back the wings and bring the head round to impale the legs on the beak.

Since there is seldom a 'bag' of them to make a main meal they are often served as a savoury and the ideal method of cooking is roasting. An oven that will keep them at a gentle sizzle is just right and they must be basted continuously with a seasoned butter (a pan of butter, with pepper and salt, on the stove is handy). Or they can be cooked in heavily buttered paper and browned off under the grill. Save the gravy in the paper. Put the bird on a sizeable piece of toasted bread and pour the buttery gravy over it.

Donald Macfarquhar's Game Pot

(Allow three days to get this dish to the table.)

A brace of young grouse	12 sprigs green heather tops
A pair of young (not small) rabbits	A finger length of stem of myrrh
	A few caraway seeds
1 lb veal	6 cloves
2 knuckles veal	12 black peppercorns
A cupful of picken cheese	Salt
3 cupfuls soft breadcrumbs	Port wine
A handful of shallots	Slices of pork fat to line the dish
A bunch of parsley	

First Day

With a very sharp knife bone the grouse to give four whole portions of breast. Then bone the legs taking great care to remove the sinews. Cut the rabbit loin in four strips and halve them; bone the legs. Go over the livers and remove the gall bag. Wash the bones, the carcasses and knuckle well and put them into the stock-pot with half a gallon of water. Add all the seasonings except the port wine.

With long boiling and careful skimming this will reduce to about half. At some point drop in the livers and give them 15 minutes only. Strain the stock through a tammy. Taste now for seasoning and remedy if necessary.

Second Day

The stock should now be a clear firm jelly. Taste it. (Hot stock and cold jellied stock often taste different). Liquify it by setting the bowl in a pan of hot water. Add the port wine judging the quantity by taste. Mince the veal and the livers and pound until smooth. Grate the cheese and add it. Melt a lump of butter in a stewpan, put in the crumbs and slowly add just enough melted stock to make a very stiff mixture. This may be all the better with a snifter of pepper and salt. Add this to the veal and cheese and work to a very well blended forcemeat.

With a very sharp knife make a slit in each breast of grouse and make as deep a pocket as possible. Fill it with forcemeat. Stuff the legs, grouse and rabbit, just by filling the cavities and folding over. Slit the pieces of loin and stuff them.

Line the game dish with the strips of pork fat, sticking them to the sides with bacon fat or lard. Do not put fat on the bottom of the dish but make a base of forcemeat. Now fill in the stuffed portions. There is a knack in this for they must be fitted in such a way that there is no fear of them 'springing' open. Fit them one piece of grouse to one piece of rabbit. Spoon stock over the mixture allowing it to soak down. Finish with a layer of forcemeat, packing it firmly down.

Put on a close fitting lid and bake in the oven for 4 hours. Do not lift the lid often but make sure that the pot is kept at boiling point and add a little more stock from time to time.

Leave overnight to get quite cold in a basin of cold well water with some salt in it.

Third Day

Again liquify the stock. There will be a good coat of lard on the pot and it will come away cleanly. Turn the pot out gently on a large ashet and spoon the liquid stock over it. Let it sit and repeat until you have a good coating of jelly. It needs no garnish but some parsley and a few sprigs of green heather tops make a fine finish.

Use a very sharp knife when carving.

Note: Picken cheese was a farmhouse cheese made with a curd which was allowed to become fairly strong then given long pressing (as much as a month) between the stones.

Cooking Ham

When selecting a ham or part of a ham for home cooking consult the grocer or butcher about the saltiness of the cut. All hams should be soaked in luke-warm water for some hours, and if really salty should be soaked for 24 hours. Time for cooking: 20 minutes to the pound and 20 minutes over.

Put the ham in a pan big enough to allow it to be covered with luke-warm water. Bring to the boil and cook gently for the required time. Take the pan away from the heat and leave the ham to cool in the water.

Skin and coat with fine brown breadcrumbs before serving.

Boiled Ham with Cider

Soak a medium-sized salted ham in cold water for 12 hours, changing the water once or twice and replacing it with luke-warm water. Scrub the ham scraping off any discoloured parts or rust and weigh it. Cover it with warm water in a roomy pot and bring it slowly to the boil skimming occasionally.

When it has boiled quite briskly for 15 minutes draw the pot away from the heat but keep it simmering. Allow 30 minutes to every pound of ham. It must never be cooked quickly as this would result in the thin end being over-cooked, the thick possibly underdone.

After about half the cooking time pour in a large bottle of cider, bring back to simmering point and finish cooking.

Leave the ham to cool in the water and when it is quite cold, skin it and trim it neatly. Coat it thickly with very fine brown breadcrumbs and stud with whole cloves.

Gammon Rasher: Colonel Cameron's Method

Cut your gammon about ½ inch thick and anywhere between ¾ lb to 1 lb in weight. Cover it with cider—draught if possible—in a shallow pan and bring slowly to the boil. Cook it gently, adding a shake of pepper and a saltspoonful of soft brown sugar, and letting it simmer for 20 minutes.

Drain it well and brush it freely with melted butter. Brander in front of a clear fire, first on one side and then on the other, until it is quite tender.

Serve with celery and sweet apples.

Note: The modern finishing method would be frying in butter, or grilling.

Baked Gammon

If possible use a piece weighing about 4 or 5 lb of an even thickness. Soak it in cold water overnight, then cook it in boiling water for 1 hour. Remove from the pan and when it cools a little remove the rind. Take a sharp pointed knife and mark the fat in diamond marks.

Put one dessertspoonful of mustard powder into a bowl, add a little water to make it into a paste, then work in 4 oz of soft brown sugar. Coat the ham with this and put it into a clean, dry baking tin. Add a cupful of cider or stock and gently cook it in a moderate oven for at least an hour. Test with a skewer at the end of that time.

To eat with baked gammon

Carrot	Chestnuts	Onion	Curry powder
Turnip	Celery	Apple	

Part cook the carrot, turnip and celery. Cut in even sized pieces. Boil the chestnuts until soft but still whole. Parboil the onion. Quarter but do not pre-cook the apple. Have all the vegetables of a size as far as possible.

Put a good knob of butter in a frying pan, lightly fry the onion and apple. Add curry powder, keep it mild. Now add the other vegetables. Cover and cook gently until all vegetables are tender. They should have been salted in first cooking.

Dish up, serve in hot dish, rice boiled and dried in another.

Ham or gammon on large platter or if the 'master' prefers it, sliced.

Crown Roast of Pork

Procure six ribs from each side of a loin of pork. Nick the ribs but do not sever them; have the bones trimmed like cutlets with quite a bit of bare bone. Now turn the pieces so that the meat is inside and the bones out. The joint will now form a circle with twelve points sticking well up. Bind securely with twine. You must have a well in the centre.

Now stuff the joint by parboiling one large onion and chopping it finely. Add 2 cupfuls of soft white breadcrumbs and 1 oz of finely shredded suet. Season with pepper and salt and 1 teaspoonful of sage. Mix into a stiff dough with milk and fill into the centre of the joint.

Pack in a piece of greaseproof paper on top of the stuffing. Twist pieces of greased paper round the points to keep them from getting too brown and place the joint in a roasting tin in which there is some melted dripping. Cook in a really hot oven: baste frequently and see that the points are not burning. After the first 20 minutes lower the heat a little, and let the meat cook evenly, allowing in all 30 minutes for every pound of pork.

While the joint is cooking, parboil 12 not very big onions and drain them well. Thirty minutes before you judge the joint will be ready impale the onions on the bones, first removing all the papers. Baste now both meat and onions until the onions are brown and juicy.

To serve, lift the joint on to a hot ashet. Strain off the fat in the roasting tin, keeping back the meat juice. Add a pint of hot water to this, add a little pepper and salt and strain it into a sauceboat.

Crown Roast of Lamb

Follow the above recipe exactly but flavour the stuffing with mint and a suspicion of rosemary; but no sage. Allow a little less time for cooking: say 20 minutes to the pound. Serve with mint sauce and red currant jelly.

Roast Leg of Pork

Score the skin thinly or ask your butcher to do this for you. Cover the joint in a roasting tin with greased paper and roast it in a hot oven; allow 25 minutes for every pound of pork. Half an hour before it is due to be dished remove the paper and baste the pork well. Give it another 30 minutes and baste frequently until the skin is crisp, brown and crackly.

Serve with a good gravy, apple sauce and sage stuffing.

Sage Stuffing

Peel and chop very finely 2 onions. Fry them in a little butter or some of the pork fat, add a cupful of soft white breadcrumbs, a dessertspoonful of chopped sage, pepper and salt. Mix well and bake in a small casserole for 15 minutes.

Apple Salad

(To eat with roast pork or roast goose)

Core the required number of good eating apples, take off a thin peeling and slice them very thinly. Put a layer into a salad bowl and dust with pepper, salt and very fine castor sugar. Sprinkle with lemon juice. Repeat until all the apples are used. Prepare just before the salad is to go to the table.

Kidneys, Bacon and Mushrooms with Mops: Colonel Cameron's Recipe

Colonel Cameron used the term 'mops' for chunky pieces of bread toasted so that they had a soft centre and they were used as mops particularly for gravy or sauce.

Take 8 lamb kidneys in their hap of suet, removing none of it, and lay them in a roasting tin. Roast in a pretty sharp oven for about thirty minutes. Take as many slices of bacon as may be desired and roll them up tightly and impale them on skewers which will fit into the roasting tin. Peel and remove the stalk from eight large meadow mushrooms.

When the kidneys are cooked remove them and cook the skewers of bacon for a little over 10 minutes, turning them once or twice. Take them out, pour off most of the fat, arrange the mushrooms in the tin, gills side up, and spoon a very little of the hot fat over them. Cover the tin with a baking sheet and cook the mushrooms in the oven until tender. Toast some slices of bread cut fairly thick.

To assemble the dish, remove the kidneys from their covering, dust lightly with pepper and the merest suspicion of salt. Take the bacon off the skewers. Carefully lift the mushrooms on to a hot ashet taking great care not to spill their liquor. Put a kidney on each mushroom, fill in the centre of the dish with the bacon rolls. Boil a tablespoonful of mushroom ketchup and a tablespoonful of warm water in the roasting tin and pour over the bacon. Arrange the mops round the side of the dish.

This is a dish for breakfast or lunch.

Note: Kidneys and mushrooms cooked in this manner also go very well with a dish of fried bacon and eggs.

Kidney and Mushroom Omelette

Cook the kidneys and the mushrooms as above then cut them up together with a sharp knife, taking care to keep all the juices. Keep hot until the omelette is cooked. Turn out the omelette on to a hot ashet, slash the top and quickly fill in the mixture. Serve at once.

Tripe

Tripe is the entrails or the large stomach of ruminating animals such as the ox. There are four different parts, the honeycomb, the book, the blanket and the monk's hood, of which the honeycomb is considered the finest. Tripe is now prepared and cooked ready for selling: the cleaning of tripe obtained straight from the slaughter-house or from a farmer who had killed an animal was a mammoth task. My own early recollection is of the start of the cleaning in a running stream, and then in successive tubs of very cold water and a scrubbing brush which was kept specially for the purpose. The initial cooking took a long time: it would be boiled for as much as 9 hours. After this it was dressed in many ways and was esteemed as a food for invalids. It was usual to parboil it, drain, and cook it again in fresh water. Some cooks liked to cook it for about 5 hours, and then change it into fresh boiling water to complete the cooking. The water from the last boiling was used in some of the dressings in subsequent dishes.

Tripe and Onions

Cut a piece of well cooked tripe into squares. Slice a couple of good sized onions and cook them in a pint of water in which the tripe was cooked, boiling until tender. The water should boil in, add half a pint of milk to it, put in the tripe, season with pepper and salt and cook for 15 minutes. Add a piece of butter and draw the pan away from the heat. Thicken with some flour blended with milk, and return to the heat; cook for a further 10 minutes.

A Baked Tripe Haggis

Line a casserole, or a terrine with a lid, with a single piece of tripe, bringing it up over the sides. Make a filling of well toasted oatmeal, finely chopped suet, finely chopped onion, at least ½ lb of liver parboiled and then minced, a good shake of black pepper and salt. Make it into a very moist mixture with some tripe stock and fill into the dish. Take another piece of tripe to fit over this, large enough to tuck down at the sides; pull the edges of the first piece over the top and pat down. Now pour over a pint of tripe stock and put the lid on the dish. Cook in a moderate oven for a little over an hour. The stock will boil away and when ready you should have a firm, not brown, haggis, top and bottom pieces being sealed together with the stuffing.

Tripe for an Invalid

Cut a piece of very well cooked tripe into tiny pieces. Pour a cupful of really good milk into a pan (or even a thin cream) and infuse a little chopped chives or parsley. Add the tripe, bring to the boil and cook gently for 10 minutes. Season with salt, thicken with a little flour blended in milk and boil for 5 minutes.

Serve with snippets of toast.

Jellied Tripe

Boil the tripe in the piece for about 5 hours. Empty the water out, cut the tripe into smallish pieces, return them to the pot with a veal knuckle or calves' feet and cover with cold water. Add an onion tied in a piece of muslin, pepper, salt and a dust of nutmeg.

Cook until very tender. Lift all of it into a basin, remove the knuckle or feet and the onion and leave to set.

6*

Brawn

1 pig's head	6 peppercorns
4 pig's feet	Salt
1 cow heel	

Wash the head and feet well and leave to steep in cold water overnight. Wash them again and put them into a roomy pot in just enough water to cover them; add the peppercorns and the salt. Cook long and gently, skimming from time to time, until the meat is falling from the bones: this may take 6 hours. Remove all the bones and the uneatable bits and cut up the meat in fine pieces.

Strain the stock, add more seasoning if you think it is required and mix in the meat; stir well and when it begins to cool set it in small bowls.

To give a little more meat two sheeps' tongues can be cooked with the head. Skin the tongues when cooked and cut them up finely.

Hare

The cooks of other days would be horrified to see a hare cut up and sold in portions for they liked to get the hare when it was freshly killed, to hang it according to their own liking and to skin it themselves. Now you can buy a portion of hare, and even hare blood in a container, but there are still many who receive a hare just as it has been killed.

The flavour improves with keeping for a short period depending on the weather: if it is cold and frosty a hare can hang a long time but if it is mild weather a few days at most. Hang it by the head in a cold dry shed or larder and see that it is protected from flies.

To Skin a Hare

Cut off the first joint of the hind and forelegs; then you will find it much more manageable if you hang it on a hook by one of the hind legs. Make a slit in the skin lengthwise over the stomach and, with the fingers, free the skin from the flesh. Draw the skin over the hind legs; pull it down over the body, the forelegs and the head. The skin should now be inside out. Use a sharp knife to sever it at the ears and the nose. Now, make a slit with a sharp knife in the stomach, lengthwise, and remove the inside. *It is important at this stage to preserve as much of the blood as possible.*

Break the membrane between the chest and the lower part of the body and if there is blood in the 'basket', i.e. the rib cavity, unhook the hare and empty it into a bowl. Remove the heart and the lungs. Slit the heart and add the blood in it to the bowl. Cut the hare into joints; the forelegs, the hind legs, saddle, basket and head.

Wash well in salted tepid water, removing all unwanted pieces of skin, the fatty tissue from the kidneys and the gall bag from the liver (if possible without breaking the bag). Dry well on a damp clean towel.

Note: A little vinegar stirred into the blood will keep it from clotting.

The portions of meat can be used in various ways: the trimmings, head, neck, basket, heart and kidneys can all be used to make soup. It was the custom in some parts of Scotland to use the trimmings and the legs for soup and then to allow the legs to become quite cold, after which they were fried or brandered. The saddle, unless it is a very old animal, roasts beautifully in a covered roasting tin if cooked gently. Make a gravy with a cupful of good stock and the same of a white wine poured into the roasting tin and seasoned.

The meat on the saddle can also be cut with a very sharp knife from the bone to form fillets which can be braised or fried. Some good stock with 2 tablespoonfuls of red currant jelly makes a delicious gravy to serve with the fillets. The legs make an excellent stew or are very good braised. A little fat bacon and a bowlful of mushrooms along with some shallots should be cooked with them.

Jugged Hare

The secret of the perfect jug is long slow cooking and discriminating flavouring. My own childhood recollection is of a heavy iron pot with a strong lid over a lazy peat fire for most of the day. Equally good was the huge earthenware cooking pot on a slow heat in the oven of a huge kitchen range. The age of the animal is not important.

Skin and paunch the hare, retaining the blood in the chest cavity and from the heart. Wash the animal well and dry it, then cut it into suitable portions. Lay them in a tureen and cover with the marinade of your choice.

Boil the head, the liver, heart and kidneys along with the basket in a stock-pot until tender: but remove the kidneys and the liver after half an hour's boiling. This will also give you as well as a stock for the jug an idea of the time the hare will take to cook. Vegetables can be added to the boiling stock but I am not in favour of this as it tends to blurr the flavour.

Leave the joints in the marinade for 24 hours. Drain them well and pat them dry in a clean towel, then toss them in flour. Heat some good roast beef or bacon fat in the cooking pot and turn the joints in it until they are set. Take them out and then fry chopped shallots or a good bowlful of onion, add a handful or so of flour and stir, then slowly add hare stock until you have a fairly thick gravy.

Beat up the blood (you may not wish to use all of it) in a fairly big bowl and beat in about half of the marinade depending on the amount there is. To this slowly add some of the thickened stock (*never* add blood mixture to stock as it would curdle).

Return to the pan, put in the joints, a sprinkling of salt, a dust of black pepper, put the lid on firmly and let it cook until almost ready.

Break up the kidneys and the liver, removing fat, string and core and rub through a sieve, mix with a cupful of port wine and a cupful of red currant jelly and stir into the pot.

Taste now for flavour; and add more salt, pepper, wine or jelly if needed.

A Farmhouse Jug

This could be a very robust affair, with oatmeal as a thickening instead of flour and haggis balls made with suet, oatmeal and blood.

Hare: Janet Murray's Method

Bone a fairly young animal, jointed, well washed and dried, cutting the meat into medium sized chunks. Cook all the bones, the blood, the heart, liver and kidneys in the stock pot, and then strain the stock on to oatmeal and make a basin of brose for the dogs.

Lightly fry the meat in butter along with a bowlful of cut up shallots but do not let this get brown. Season with white pepper, salt and a teaspoonful of lemon rind, and cover with cream. Cook most gently, almost at simmering point, until the meat is well on its way to being ready. Add another cupful of cream, a cupful of button mushrooms and a cupful of shelled chestnuts.

Serve with snippets of toast.

Rabbit

No amount of cooking or flavouring will disguise 'that rabbity flavour' if the source of it is not removed either when the animal is being skinned or washed following skinning.

At the tail there is a very small piece of membrane that gives the unpleasant flavour: even a pinhead of this membrane can cause trouble and few cooks know how to look for it. Examine the tail of the rabbit; you may find a tiny piece of the membrane on either side of it. It is green in colour and removing it is more important than any other part of the preparation.

Jellied Rabbit

1 young rabbit
Small piece of ham end
4 sheets gelatine or ½ oz
   powdered gelatine

Pepper, salt and a small piece
   of mace
A slice or two of onion
1 pint water
2 eggs

Wash, dry and joint a young rabbit. Cook it slowly in the oven in a cooking pot or pie-dish with all the other ingredients or steam it in a pan until the meat is tender. Keep the gravy up to a pint, adding more water if necessary. Hard boil the 2 eggs, shell and slice them, and arrange them in a mould.

Take all the meat from the bones and cut it into small pieces. Arrange on top of the egg and then strain the liquor over it, having tasted it to see if more seasoning is required. Remember that the ham may be a little salty and make allowance accordingly.

Leave until the next day before turning out and serving with lettuce.

Cream of Rabbit

A young rabbit
1 onion
Parsley
Pepper and salt

1 egg and a cupful of cream
Water
2 oz butter
Heaped tablespoonful of flour

Joint the rabbit and wash and dry the joints. Melt the butter in a stewpan, add the flour and cook it a little; then slowly add fully ½ pint of warm water. Stir until the sauce is quite smooth and then add the parsley and the onion sliced.

Add the rabbit, bring it through the boil and let it cook gently until tender. If it is a young rabbit it should cook in an hour or less and when it is quite cooked take it out and bone it. Strain the sauce and bring it to the boil again. Beat the egg in a roomy bowl, add the cream and pour the boiling sauce over it, beating vigorously the while. Return to the pan and stir until it 'takes' but on no account let it come through the boil.

Place the rabbit on a hot ashet and pour the sauce over it.

Rabbit Curry: Colonel Cameron's Recipe

Joint, wash and dry well the required amount of rabbit. Lightly brown the joints in a nugget of good beef dripping in an iron stew pan. Lift them out and in the same fat fry two large sliced onions and one large tart apple also sliced. (In season green gooseberries can be substituted for the apple).

Turn lightly until brown then lay the pieces of rabbit on top. Add 6 cloves, a small piece of root ginger bruised, about a dozen peppercorns, a tablespoonful of dessicated coconut and, if you have a fresh coconut, add the milk to the mixture, 2 tablespoonfuls of chutney, a pint of good gravy, a tablespoonful of curry powder, black pepper and salt.

Cook until the meat is tender, then lift out the joints, strain the gravy into a bowl and wash and dry the pan. Put the pan on the heat again with a good knob of butter, let it sizzle for a minute then add a good spoonful of flour, and cook it for a minute. Now add the stock and bring to the boil. Add more seasoning if necessary, especially curry.

Take all the meat from the bones, cut it into small pieces, add these to the sauce and add a cupful of well-washed sultanas. Bring to the boil and cook gently for 15 minutes.

Serve with a border of boiled rice.

Boiled Rice: Colonel Cameron's Recipe

Drop the whole rice into a pan of fast boiling water so that the grains swirl round. The water must be well salted, with a spoonful of lemon juice and a sliver or two of rind for flavour. Cook for 15 minutes and test between the fingers. It is ready when there should be just a suggestion of hard core.

Turn the rice into a sieve in the sink and run the cold tap over it. Put the sieve on the rack of the kitchen range and turn the rice with a spoon until it is dry and every grain separate.

Raised Rabbit Pie

Paste

1 lb plain white flour
6 oz lard

A good pinch of salt
½ pint milk and water mixed

Filling

2 rabbits
Piece of ham or mutton
3 eggs

2 sheets gelatine or a teaspoonful of powdered gelatine

Be very exact in your quantities for the paste: sift the flour and the salt into a baking bowl. Bring the lard, the milk and the water to the boil in a saucepan. Pour the boiling liquid into the bowl and stir the mixture into a firm dough. As soon as it can be handled work it until it is smooth but on no account allow it to cool (once cold it is impossible to line a mould with it).

At the time when this recipe would be used frequently many kitchens had a raised pie mould, perhaps a range of them. They were embossed with a pattern and hinged. The join was held by a pin and when the pin was removed the two sides swung back and the pie could be easily removed. Where a raised mould is not available, a cake tin with a movable bottom is a good substitute.

Grease the mould thoroughly with lard, making sure that the pin which holds it together is secure and that the bottom is properly in position. Take two thirds of the paste to line the mould and keep the other part for the lid. Keep the piece for the lid warm by setting the basin with the paste in it in a larger basin with warm water and cover with a towel.

Now take the larger piece, work it firmly into the shape of the mould, working with the thumbs to get it quite to the top, and making sure the bottom is quite flat. (This is important: the pie must sit evenly when it comes to the table).

The rabbit must be cooked beforehand so that the meat can be taken from the bones. Cook it with a piece of mutton or ham end (remember the ham may be salty so make allowance for this). Add at least 2 pints of water.

When cold enough to handle, remove all the meat from the bones and cut into smallish portions. Fill into the mould along with the whole eggs hard-boiled and shelled into the pie. Strain enough of the liquor over the meat to half fill the mould.

Roll out the paste for the lid and fit it neatly on. Pinch the edges well together, leaving a little 'slack'. Cut this slack with a scissors at $\frac{1}{4}$-inch intervals. Twist the cut parts, alternately to the right and the left. With the odds and ends of paste not used cut some leaves to decorate the top of the pie. Make two good slits in the centre, crosswise, twist back the points and arrange the leaves above the points. Brush with beaten egg.

Place in a really hot oven for 15 minutes, then lower the heat and cook for 1 hour. Melt the gelatine and put it into the rest of the rabbit liquor. Bring to the boil and fill it into the pie from time to time during cooking. Do not let it overflow as this would make the paste sodden.

Serve cold.

Sweetbreads

Sweetbreads are a delicacy but only if very carefully prepared. They must be blanched irrespective of later cooking and can be very greasy unless all the fat is removed. Wash them well in cold water and then soak them for an hour in cold salted water. Wash them again, put them in a saucepan, cover them with cold water and bring the water slowly to the boil. Cook for 10 minutes, then run the cold tap on them. Remove all skin, fat and membrane and they are now ready for final cooking.

For an invalid it is better to stew them. Cover them with milk in the saucepan, add a tiny piece of butter, a sprig of parsley and a little salt. Cook until the sweetbread is tender—this usually takes about an hour—but it could take less. When cooked it should divide easily with a fork. Remove the parsley, thicken the sauce with a spoonful of flour blended with a little milk.

Serve with a border of fresh green peas and toast.

Fried Sweetbreads

Parboil, cool and trim away all fat and membrane. Cook in stock or water until tender, then press between two plates. When quite cold, cut into individual portions, coat with egg and dip in brown breadcrumbs. Fry until a pale golden brown in deep fat.

French beans or green peas go well with this dish as do well fried crisp potato chips. The stock in which the sweetbreads were cooked can be used to make a sauce with chopped parsley.

Roast Gigot (January 1852)

Take a shovel and bring all the glowing fire to the front; fill in the back with fresh fuel and pack the front by putting in small pieces where there are gaps. Make sure that the fire is drawing well for if it stay not bright and clear the joint may well turn sour instead of cooking.

Look to the joint. Wipe it well with a cloth wrung out of vinegar. Scrape any parts with a knife if necessary. Take off the knuckle bone and trim away any piece of flank that may spoil the shape of the joint. Put the roasting screen in front of the fire, with the dripping pan under it, and a long basting ladle in a pan beside it.

Fix the jack on the hook under the mantlepiece and let the gigot come to rest close to the fire. Baste it with some melted dripping and give it 5 to 10 minutes to brown and seal the skin.

After that, draw it back according to the heat and allow it 20 minutes to the pound of meat. It may take longer but it is easy to judge after the basic cooking time, indeed it is necessary to see that the basic cooking time itself is not too long—this depends entirely on the age of the animal. It must be basted steadily at intervals during cooking and some hold that every 10 minutes is not too much.

If available a skin of suet can be wrapped round the joint and this lessens the need for continual basting. *But,* make no mistake, the secret of a juicy joint, mutton, beef, venison or even bullock's heart, is basting, and roasting not too quick and not too slow. Unhook the joint when it is cooked and lay it on a heated ashet. Pour the dripping gently into a bowl, leaving the gravy in the pan, which will be served with the meat. A few globules of fat are an attraction, much fat an abomination.

Before putting on the table, put a frill round the knuckle.

Roast Gigot of Mutton

Choose a small gigot of mutton or lamb—but make sure you know which it is—lamb will take much less cooking. Put the joint into a roasting tin, add just a little fat and place in a hot oven. Give it about 20 minutes in a really hot oven, then lower the heat a little and cook, allowing 20 minutes to the pound of meat and 20 minutes over.

Once upon a time a joint had to be basted continually but with the electric oven, or gas oven, it is possible to get an even, steady roasting temperature which does away with much of the basting.

The meat can also be cooked in a covered tin, or in a cover of tin foil which allows the fat and steam to run continuously over the meat.

Stuffing a Gigot

Get the butcher to remove the bone; stuff the cavity with the stuffing given for shoulder. Serve with gravy, red currant jelly and mint sauce. Serve caper sauce with boiled mutton.

Hot-Pot

A hot-pot can be delectable and gives much scope for personal choice. It can be made with mutton, potatoes and onions only or it can have lambs' kidneys, mushrooms, new peas and carrots added to that.

2 to 3 lb middle neck of mutton	2 lamb kidneys
2 lb potatoes	$\frac{1}{2}$ lb mushrooms
2 onions	Pepper and salt

Peel the potatoes and cut them in thick chunks. Cut the mutton into chops. Parboil the onions and slice them. Peel the mushrooms, and the kidneys: cut the latter in half, removing any fatty core. Put some good dripping into a stew pan. Brown the pieces of mutton lightly then take them out and keep them hot. Lightly fry the onion and the kidneys, remove them also, and just set the mushrooms.

Place the ingredients in a large casserole in layers, adding pepper and salt as you go. Almost cover with hot stock, put a lid on the casserole and cook gently for 2 hours, taking care that it does not boil in. Peas and young carrots can be added after an hour's cooking.

Mutton Chops with Chestnuts

To 6 chops allow ½ lb chestnuts and 3 medium sized onions. Make a slit in the skin of the chestnuts and put them in a warm oven until the skin comes off easily. Parboil the onions and slice them. Trim the chops. Fry the onions lightly in some fat, not more than a dessertspoonful, in a hot pan. Then remove them and let them sit in a strainer as they do pick up a lot of fat.

Now brown the chops first on one side and then on the other: pour off the fat and add 1 pint of warm water or a not very strong stock. Add the onions, and the chestnuts and season with pepper, salt and a few crumbs of dried mint.

Put the lid on and cook gently for 2 hours.

Serve with mashed potatoes and a green vegetable.

Shoulder of Mutton, Stuffed

To stuff a shoulder or a loin of mutton ask your butcher to bone it but not roll it. Spread the meat the skin side down on a board. With a broad knife spread the stuffing evenly over the meat but do not go too near the edge.

Roll up firmly, and bind with fine twine. Roast as for a gigot, allowing 25 minutes to the pound and 20 minutes over.

Stuffing

½ teaspoonful chopped mint	2 tablespoonfuls finely shredded
4 tablespoonfuls fine white	suet
breadcrumbs	1 teaspoonful chopped parsley
1 onion	Pepper and salt
	1 egg, a little milk if necessary

Parboil the onion and chop it finely. Mix all the ingredients together with the beaten egg and add milk only if necessary. The stuffing should be firm and moist and not crumbly.

Irish Stew

The meat for this can be left-over cooked mutton, uncooked scrag end, or even cutlets.

Mutton	Butter or dripping
Onions	Pepper and salt
Potatoes	

Peel and parboil the onions, fry them lightly in the fat and then remove them from the pan. Now put in the mutton cut in small pieces (unless you are using cutlets) and brown in the fat. Put back the onions, add the potatoes, sliced, a little stock, put on the lid, and cook until the meat is ready.

Season with pepper and salt before dishing.

Beef Udder

Udder, known in Scots dialect as 'Lure', was regarded as a delicacy. The butcher reserved this for special customers and was able to give a guide as to the length of time it would take to cook.

A favourite method was to cook it long and slowly in a stock with onions and to serve it sliced with an onion sauce. If from an old animal it was cooked in salted water with a spoonful of vinegar added and served cold with a green vegetable. Calf's udder was valued as a forcemeat for stuffing fowls.

A Stew of Lamb or Mutton

A piece of mutton or lamb that can be cut into individual pieces is most suitable for this recipe.

1 tablespoonful good dripping	A piece of turnip
2 onions	2 carrots

Parboil and slice the onions. Wash and pare the carrots and turnip and cut them into portions. Trim surplus fat off the mutton and cut into portions also.

Heat the dripping in the stew pan and gently fry the onion in it. Lift it out and let it strain into a bowl so that it is not greasy. Put the mutton into the pan, keep turning it until it is brown and then pour off the fat. Put back the onions, add the other vegetables, season well with pepper and salt and add half a pint of hot water.

Bring to the boil and let this cook gently for at least 2 hours testing to see if the meat is tender. Make up the gravy if it has boiled in, thicken it with a spoonful of flour, add more seasoning if necessary and serve with mashed potatoes.

Braising

The oven pot, used where no oven was available, was a strong iron pot with a firmly fitting iron lid. In some cases the lid was 'dished' (made with troughs that could take hot peats) and was ideal for cooking fowls, game birds and large pieces of meat; this was termed 'braising'. It allowed long steady cooking, and in the more sophisticated kitchens where there were stoves and ovens one could find the same idea in the braising pan. This was a heavyware pan, not unlike a fish kettle in shape, with a tight fitting lid like a small bath, which was filled with live charcoal, thus the cooking was from above as well as from below.

To braise meat or fowls cream or butter was used freely together with strips of bacon, and small pieces of vegetable such as onion, celery and meadow mushrooms. Interesting flavouring was added, perhaps a blade or two of mace, a corner of nutmeg, a sprig of sage and that fail-me-never, parsley.

Birds in particular took on a rich golden brown in the braising pan and were moist and tender when cooked. The tendency to serve game birds almost underdone is a modern trend, and far from an improvement in the opinion of the gourmet.

Braised Grouse

This is a very old Scots method of cooking pheasant, partridge and grouse. It is particularly good when the bird is not young. The grouse should be plucked, drawn and singed and lightly washed in tepid water. Then dry it very well and fix it with skewers.

Put a spoonful of butter into a roomy pot with a close fitting lid. Heat it and turn the bird in it for a minute before putting in a cupful of cream, a little black pepper, a little salt and a small piece of whole mace. Put the lid on and braise for about 20 minutes before lifting the lid. From time to time add more cream until the bird is cooked.

When ready to serve, the bird should be brown and juicy and there should be a most delicious sauce.

Ravioli

This recipe is dated 1892 and states: 'It requires some assembling.' The paste used for ravioli is *nouille* paste and depends much on good kneading.

The Paste

½ lb flour
3 egg yolks
A pinch of salt

A tablespoonful of very cold water

Sift the flour with the salt and make it into a paste with the beaten yolks and the cold water. Use your judgment as to the amount of water required. Knead the dough long and carefully until it is very smooth and then let it rest for an hour. To use it divide it evenly into two and roll out both pieces very thinly.

Filling

3 egg yolks	1 tablespoonful grated cheese
Breast of a fowl, cooked	1 dessertspoonful chopped
4 oz cooked ham	parsley
The blanched brains of a calf	Pepper and salt

First put the fowl meat and ham through a very fine mincer then pound it until smooth in a bowl. Add the brains, the yolks of eggs, the cheese, parsley and pepper and salt. Form into balls a little bigger than a walnut.

Lay out one piece of paste, brush it lightly with cold water and arrange the forcemeat in rows, just under two inches apart. Lay the other piece of paste on top and press it firmly between the rows, sealing each ball of forcemeat in a little packet. Cover with a clean towel and leave for an hour.

To cook the ravioli, bring a wide pan of salted water or fine white stock to the boil. Set a pan with a cup of good brown sauce on the stove and another with a cup of tomato sauce. Have a couple of spoonfuls of grated cheese to hand, a fireproof dish and a fish slice.

When the water is boiling, cut each ravioli in a square with a pastry cutter. When all are cut, drop them into the pan and boil briskly for exactly 2 minutes: then let them simmer for 8 minutes. Lift them out with the fish slice and drain on a clean towel.

Arrange them in layers in the fireproof dish, sprinkle the cheese over them, then pour the hot brown sauce over them and then the tomato sauce. Place the dish in a hot oven for 5 or 6 minutes.

(Use the whites of the eggs to make a supply of meringues when the oven is cooling.)

Sauces

Sauces

Many years ago I bought a cookery book at a sale. It was dated 1892 and in the inner page was the crest of one of our Scottish houses. There were about a dozen pages at the end for notes and, curiously enough, they were filled with recipes for making sauces.

In a very firm even writing is the following: 'Cook taught me to make sauce this morning. There was a huge fire in the kitchen range and it was very warm although there was ice on the milk pans in the larder.'

Sauce should be smooth and well-seasoned, and can today be made by the pint and kept in the refrigerator. However, here are the quantities for ½ pint of white sauce:

2 oz butter	½ pint of liquid, which need not
1½ oz plain white flour	necessarily be milk

Melt the butter in a saucepan, let it come to the point when it sizzles but do not brown it. Then put in the flour and cook it a little in the butter. Have it thoroughly incorporated with the flour before adding the liquid slowly, beating all the time.

Liquid for sauce need not be heated but if it is warmed a little the sauce thickens more quickly and there is less fear of it burning. No sauce is ready the moment it comes to the boil: it must cook for at least 5 minutes to take away the raw taste of the flour.

Season according to its use.

Brown Sauce (using a meat cube)

Take the same proportions and make ½ pint of liquid with a part or whole of a meat or chicken cube according to size and the strength of flavour required. Brown the butter a little in this case, add the flour, then the warm, but not boiling, liquid and cook.

Liquids for Sauce

Liquids can be infused beforehand. Milk for sauces can be put on to simmer gently with the flavour required. Small pieces of onion, a clove of garlic, herbs, celery, cloves, mace, peppercorns, can all be used to flavour milk. Milk or water in which fish has been cooked can make an excellent foundation to go with fish dishes.

When raw eggs or egg yolks are to be added beat them in a roomy bowl and pour the warm sauce over them, beating vigorously the while.

Note: Egg sauces do not keep long by the fire without spoiling. Cream should be added at the very last minute before serving.

It cannot be stressed too strongly that a sauce must be smooth, well cooked and well seasoned. The proportions for seasoning cannot be laid down in a hard and fast rule. Much depends on the dish for which the sauce is required. As a guide, here are some of the flavourings:

Anchovy essence	Celery
Shrimps	Mushrooms
Fish trimmings	Chestnuts
Lobster coral	Hard-boiled eggs
Mustard	Horseradish
Capers	Tomato
Oysters	Thyme
Onions	Mint
Garlic	Mace
Parsley	

Hard-boiled eggs should be chopped finely and added at the last minute. Mustard should be blended with a little milk and added after the sauce has come to the boil. Tomato juice can be obtained by slicing tomatoes and setting them in a pan in a not too hot part of the cooker. Strain and add to the sauce just before dishing. When cooking with cloves, stick them into a piece of onion.

Apple Sauce

Slice 4 large cooking apples and put them into a saucepan with just enough water to cover them, and 2 cloves. Cook them to a pulp and then put them through a sieve. Put 1 oz of butter in the pan, add the pulped apples, 1 tablespoonful of sugar, a pinch of salt and a teaspoonful of lemon juice.

Bring to the boil and it is ready to serve.

Caper Sauce

Infuse ½ pint of milk with a slice of onion and strain it. Melt 2 oz of butter in a saucepan, and then stir in 1½ oz of flour until the butter and flour are well mixed. Then slowly add the strained milk, stirring all the time. Let it boil for 5 minutes at least.

Chop 1 tablespoonful of capers a little and work them into the sauce with pepper and salt to taste. Add a few grains of sugar and 1 dessertspoonful of the vinegar from the caper bottle. Do not boil after this.

Brandy and Almond Sauce

This is best when made just when it is going to be used.

2 oz castor sugar
4 oz fresh butter
3 dessertspoonfuls brandy

1 heaped tablespoonful ground almonds

Beat the butter and sugar to a cream and then beat in the ground almonds and finally the brandy.

Brandy Sauce

Beat ¼ lb of butter with 3 oz of soft brown sugar until it is light and creamy. Slowly add ½ a glass of brandy.

Bread Sauce

Pour ½ pint of milk into a saucepan, add some slices of onion, a blade or two of mace, and 6 peppercorns. Set this over a slow heat to infuse (this will take about 30 minutes). Stir from time to time to see that it does not singe.

Turn a wire sieve upside down on a sheet of kitchen paper and rub enough white bread through it to give 2 cupfuls of crumbs. Strain the sauce milk and return it to the pan. Add about a dessert-spoonful of butter, and bring the milk to the boil. When it is actually boiling add the crumbs, place a lid on the pan and set aside for 10 minutes. Stir it gently, add more pepper and salt to taste and bring to the boil again.

Bread sauce should be served with game or poultry.

Miss Mary's Butter Sauce

This is a soft velvety sauce to serve with fish—particularly sole—and vegetables.

½ oz butter
1 oz flour
1¼ gills water
1 dessertspoonful lemon juice

1 teaspoonful finely grated
  lemon rind
4 to 5 teaspoonfuls butter
Salt

Infuse the lemon rind in the water. If you let the water boil in make it up again to 1¼ gills when you strain it. Melt the ½ oz of butter in a saucepan and slowly add the flour. Cook a little then begin to add the water, stirring well. Add the salt and let the sauce cook at this stage for 5 minutes.

Now begin to put in the teaspoonfuls of butter, one at a time, letting the sauce cook gently. Take it away from the heat and add the lemon juice. Serve at once.

Celery Sauce

Part of a head of celery
2 oz butter
1½ oz plain white flour

1 cup cream
1 cup liquor in which the celery
  is cooked

Trim and wash the celery and cut it into small pieces. Cook it until it is tender in slightly salted water. Strain it. Melt the butter in the saucepan and stir in the flour.

Cook it a little and then slowly add the cupful of celery water. Cook for a few minutes, then add the cream, a little pepper, more salt if necessary and the strained celery.

Serve with poultry and white fish.

Cheese Sauce

1 pint milk	4 oz grated cheese
3 oz flour	Pepper, salt and mustard
4 oz butter	

Melt the butter in a saucepan and stir in the flour allowing it to cook a little. Then slowly add the milk which could be heated a little but not to boiling point. Season with pepper, salt and a spoonful of mustard and allow to cook for 10 minutes. Now fold in the grated cheese but do not return it to the heat.

This sauce should be smooth, rich and creamy and can be used to coat cauliflower, or hardboiled eggs. Boiled macaroni can be added to it and baked to make MACARONI AND CHEESE. Sprinkle on top a mixture of crumbs and grated cheese.

Curry Sauce

1 large cooking apple	1 dessertspoonful chutney
1 large onion	1 tablespoonful grated coconut
1 oz butter	A saltspoonful ground ginger
1 dessertspoonful curry powder	A saltspoonful sugar
1 dessertspoonful flour	A cup of cream
$\frac{1}{2}$ pint good stock	Pepper and salt

Parboil and chop the onion finely; chop the apple without peeling or coring it and fry lightly in the butter. Add the curry powder and then the flour. Thicken this with the stock and bring to the boil. Add all the other ingredients except the cream and cook for 30 minutes.

Strain, add more seasoning if necessary and pour in the cream just before serving.

Miss Mary's Cu'cummer Sauce

Beat a cupful of thick cream until it is set—but not stiff. Slowly work in 2 tablespoonfuls of vinegar, a pinch of salt and a pinch of castor sugar. Then fold in a cupful of grated cucumber.

This sauce is delicious with salmon.

Miss Mary's Mint Sauce

1 cupful finely chopped fresh
green mint
1 tablespoonful brown sugar

½ cup boiling water
3 tablespoonfuls wine vinegar

Chop the mint finely and put it in a bowl. Add the sugar and cover with the boiling water. Leave until quite cold, then add the vinegar.

Mayonnaise Sauce

3 yolks of eggs
2 gills salad oil

1 tablespoonful vinegar
Pepper and salt

Break the yolks into a bowl and season with pepper and salt. Stir them well with a wooden spoon and then add the oil, drop by drop. After some oil has been added it can be put in a little quicker, but not too hurriedly as the oil must be incorporated with the egg.

The sauce should be smooth with the consistency of thick cream and of a velvety texture. Start adding the vinegar slowly when about two thirds of the oil has been added.

Boiled Dressing (for fish, ham and cheese)

2 dessertspoonfuls flour
2 teaspoonfuls mustard
2 teaspoonfuls sugar
1 teaspoonful salt
A good shake of pepper

½ pint milk
2 eggs
2 tablespoonfuls butter
2 tablespoonfuls vinegar

Mix the flour, mustard, sugar, pepper and salt and blend slowly and smoothly with the milk. Beat the 2 eggs and add them, and then dissolve the butter and add it. Last, pour in the vinegar.

Set the bowl in a pan of boiling water and stir continuously in one direction only until it thickens. On no account let this mixture come to the boil or it will curdle.

Serve when perfectly cold. It will keep for some time bottled.

Cranberry Sauce

1 lb cranberries   4 oz sugar
1-2 gills water

Wash the cranberries and put them in a pan with the water and add the sugar. Bring to the boil and cook to a pulp. Rub through a sieve. If too thick add a little more water.

Cranberry sauce can be served with turkey, chicken and mutton.

Caramel

4 oz sugar   Juice of two lemons, strained

Put the juice and the sugar into a strong saucepan, melt the sugar and stir until the mixture becomes a pale golden brown.

To use, pour it into a pudding bowl, then roll the caramel round and round the bowl until it firms.

To bottle caramel, put a cupful of sugar into a hot pan and stir until it melts and then turns a pale brown. Slowly add a cupful of very hot water and bring through the boil. Boil for a minute or two and bottle when cool.

Syrup Sauce

Melt 1 oz of butter in a saucepan and add 1 oz of flour. Cook the flour for a minute then slowly add ½ pint of water. Stir until the sauce comes to the boil and cook for 3 minutes before adding a large tablespoonful of syrup and a few drops of lemon essence.

Treacle Sauce

Make as for syrup but do not add lemon.

Sherry Custard Sauce

2 yolks of eggs	1 oz castor sugar
2 gills milk	½ glass sherry

Beat the yolks with the sugar. Bring the milk to the boil and pour over the yolks and sugar, beating vigorously the while. Put the mixture in the bowl into a pan of boiling water and stir until it coats the spoon. Do not allow it to curdle. Slowly add the sherry.

A Useful Sauce

In a pint of good stock cook a piece of carrot, turnip, onion, 1 tomato, some scraps of lean ham, a sliver of mace, 6 peppercorns, a couple of cloves, and a bunch of parsley. Cook until the vegetables are soft and strain. Do not rub any of the vegetables through the sieve.

Measure and make up to a pint if it has boiled in. Return to the pan and add ½ gill of sherry, ½ gill of wine vinegar and boil this slowly until it is down to half.

Brown 1 oz of butter in a saucepan and then add 1 oz of flour and cook. Slowly add the stock, now cooled a little, bring to the boil and season with pepper, salt and a little sugar to taste.

Sweet Melted Butter: Mima's Recipe

Melt 1 oz of butter in a small saucepan and then stir in 1 oz of flour. Cook it a little then pour in a gill of water and stir until it boils. Now add a tablespoonful of syrup, a little lemon juice and bring the whole to a pouring consistency with rum.

Aspic Jelly

Good cooks kept a supply of aspic jelly which was used as a coating, a garnish or a liquid in which cooked poultry, game or fish could be set. In some kitchens it was made from the long cooking of veal knuckles, calves' feet and ham bones with shallots. This was boiled until reduced to one third, then cleared and seasoned.

The seasoning depended on the intended use—the jelly for fish would be quite different from that for pheasant or venison.

The following recipe is a quick method and quite a supply can be made with these ingredients and proportions. French leaf gelatine was the most favoured and was cut up and added without further preparation; but if powdered gelatine is used it is advisable to mix it with some cold water before adding to the cooking pot.

1½ pints water	A piece of carrot, celery and
¼ pint wine or tarragon vinegar	2 shallots
¼ pint cooking sherry	Salt
Rind and juice of 2 lemons	2 eggs
1 dozen whole peppercorns	1 oz gelatine to each pint of
A sprig of parsley	liquid

Cook the vegetables, peppercorns and lemon rind in the water until the vegetables are tender. Strain and make up to the original quantity. Allow to cool before returning to the pan.

Wash the eggs well in cold water, separate the yolks from the whites and beat the whites sufficiently to froth them but no more. Add this to the liquid along with the shells finely crushed. Pour in the lemon juice, the sherry and the vinegar and put the pan over a slow heat. (A deepish pan is preferable as the liquid rises when it boils.) With a whisk beat it until it does come to the boil. Bring it to the top of the pan at least three times, drawing it away from the heat after each rising. Taste it now for salt and add a little more if you think it necessary.

Strain through a flannel bag into a warm bowl. (It may have to go through the bag more than once to clear it properly.) Set and use as necessary.

Seasoning

Fish—dill, leaf savoury, parsley, nutmeg sparingly
Chicken—thyme, parsley, rosemary, mace
Game—mace, clove, tarragon, celery seed, nutmeg
Pork—caraway, sage

Aspic Mayonnaise

4 tablespoonfuls mayonnaise in ½ pint aspic jelly

Add the jelly to the mayonnaise, not vice versa.

'Picken' Sauce (Piquant)

1 oz plain white flour
1 oz sugar
1 tablespoonful treacle
1 quart vinegar

1 teaspoonful salt
1 teaspoonful mustard
Black pepper
1 tablespoonful cold water

Mix the dry ingredients well then mix to a paste with the cold water. Now add the treacle and the vinegar and cook in a double pan. If you do not have a double pan, put on a saucepan with warm water. Set the bowl in this and stir the sauce—one way only—until it coats the back of a spoon. The sauce itself must not boil.

A good relish for cold beef, it is also very good with potted head.

Speciality of the House

Paté and Terrines

A cunning in blending flavours, long cooking and skilful presentation were the first considerations for paté and terrines. Many cooks in Scottish castles excelled at them but kept their knowledge a close secret: it goes without saying that they had the pick of the game larder when a game paté or terrine was on the menu.

We are apt to think of paté as a smooth blend of many ingredients into a paste, but it is also a dish of pieces of meat, game, veal, fish and chicken cooked long and slowly. Some gourmets hold that rabbit, in a paté, is superior to chicken. There was a distinct knack in packing in the pieces so that they fitted closely together.

Much fat figured in many of the recipes in the form of butter, lard or bacon fat. Indeed, some of the terrines are lined with strips of bacon fat. Flavourings are legion: port wine, vinegars of various flavour, garlic, parsley, thyme, sage, mint, red currant jelly, rowan liqueur, Madeira to mention but a few.

Great pains were taken in the making of the sauce in which the paté was to be cooked: a strong stock was made with game, chicken, and perhaps lamb or ham bones, and flavoured with thyme, bay leaves and parsley.

Shallots were much used but not in the stock; they were finely cut up and fried in butter in a saucepan. Flour was added to this and cooked then the strained stock was put in and when cooked was flavoured with wine. This was a smooth velvety sauce rather like a cream consistency.

If gelatine was being used ½ an ounce was allowed for each pint of stock. The stock was also used to moisten forcemeat to go into the terrine and the pieces of meat, game, veal, or chicken were 'set' and no more in a frying pan before the dish was assembled. The sauce was on the strong side as far as flavouring was concerned since it lost a little when cold.

In addition to forcemeat, hard-boiled eggs, whole, tiny button mushrooms, chestnuts and even olives would be added. In season plovers' eggs were a great delicacy and were used along with chicken and veal paté very delicately flavoured. Individual choice ranged from turkey to bantam's eggs as many 'favourite' recipes reveal.

At Slains Castle where Dr. Johnson and Boswell spent a night there was a family recipe, called receipt, for a cold fish platter which had several kinds of fish and when in season gulls' eggs, crab meat, and fine dilse which had been crisped over a clear fire on an iron made for that purpose. With this was served a tureen of mayonnaise sauce with 'bites' in it, such as chopped celery, or walnuts. Crocks of gulls' eggs were preserved for baking but not allowed fine enough to serve whole.

Another famous house on that particular part of the coast had a receipt, a closely guarded secret, for a terrine of leveret, goose eggs, with a forcemeat of the liver with grapes and shallots, the stock being lightly flavoured with mace and a wine.

The forcemeat was as important if not more so than the main body of the dish. It was made from pieces of the meats to be used put through a fine mincer once or even twice and then pounded until very smooth. Breadcrumbs, well moistened with the stock and seasoned, were added. Some cooks liked to make a mixture of breadcrumbs, butter and stock in a saucepan over a gentle heat until the mixture left the sides and bottom of the pan cleanly. This was added to the pounded meat. The usual arangement was a base, even a lining of forcemeat, with the main ingredients bedded down in it.

The dish had to be closely covered and where the casserole or terrine had a lid it was luted down with a strong paste of flour and water.

The time allowed for cooking was at least 3 hours gentle cooking and if the dish was to be kept for some time it was essential to see that it was thoroughly cooled, perhaps in a bath of ice, salt and water.

Beetroot in Sauce

Wash 6 beets. Do not use a knife; for if you cut them in any way they 'bleed' and lose all their colour. Boil them in salted water until they are tender. Pour off the boiling water, put the pan under the cold tap and, with the fingers, bruise off the skin. Dice the beet.

For the sauce, put 2 tablespoonfuls of sugar and 1 dessert-spoonful of cornflour in a saucepan and add 2 tablespoonfuls of vinegar. Stir until the mixture boils. Stir in a good knob of butter then mix in the beet. Keep warm but do not boil again.

Mrs Gibson's Paté

1 lb lean steak, cut into cubes	2 shallots sliced
½ lb lean ham, cut likewise	1 tablespoonful anchovy sauce
½ lb liver bought in a piece and also cut into cubes	A blade of mace
	A spray of parsley

Butter a steaming bowl, place the mace and the shallots in the bottom of the bowl and cover with the parsley. Fill the well-mixed cubes into the bowl and add 1 tablespoon of water. Cover with buttered paper or a well-fitting lid and steam steadily for 3 hours.

Mince the meats in a fine blade mincer, keeping back the other ingredients. Then pound the minced meat in a mortar until it is smooth.

Now start the seasoning by adding salt, black pepper, the anchovy sauce and, when you think the flavour is just right, 6 oz of softened butter.

Press very firmly into small pots, leaving no air space, cover to the very edges with melted butter and store in a cold larder.

Note: The butter or lard cover on paté must seal with the edges of the pot.

Brose

There are many variations of brose but the basic recipe is oatmeal thickened with a boiling liquid.

Place 2 handfuls of oatmeal in a bowl, add salt and a knob of butter, and pour on sufficient boiling water to thicken the meal, stirring rapidly all the time. Brose is eaten with syrup, treacle, milk, buttermilk or ale according to taste.

The best bowl for making brose is the wooden bowl or brose caup, known in some districts as a bicker, and the individual bowl is 'turned' so that a man could hold it in the palm of one hand while stirring with the other. Brose caups or bickers were a great feature of the Timmer Market in Aberdeen and the buyer usually tested it for size with the breadth of his hand. Such a caup would easily hold about 3 pints of liquid. A larger one was bought, once in a lifetime, to go into the meal girnal; this was known as the girnal bassie.

Athole Brose (1)

Athole brose differs from ordinary brose in that there is no heat needed. Place 1 tablespoonful of freshly ground oatmeal into a jug and stir in a tumblerful of cold well water. Put a large tablespoonful of run honey into a large bowl and slowly mix in the water off the meal until it is as thick as cream, stirring well. Now pour in 3 large glasses of whisky (toddy whisky preferably) mix well and it is ready to use.

Athole Brose (2)

Dissolve 1 lb of dripped honey in a basin of cold water; stir with a silver or horn spoon. When the honey and water are thoroughly mixed add by degrees 1½ pints of good whisky, stirring briskly until a froth rises.

Bottle and cork tightly.

Kail Brose

Kail brose is made with oatmeal, the liquor from a pan of boiling kail, salt, pepper and a lump of butter.

Milk Brose

Milk brose, often called Knotty Tam, is made with boiling milk and a handful of oatmeal plunged in. The aim is large mealy lumps which are still dry in the centre, mealy cores being a great treat.

Cadger's Brose

Cadger's brose is made like milk brose, the liquid being boiling water.

Neep (Turnip) Brose

Neep brose is made as kail brose with the bree from a pan of boiling turnip.

Beremeal Porridge

Have the water for the porridge at the boil. Mix the beremeal with a little water and then pour it into the boiling water, stirring vigorously all the time. Season with salt and keep on stirring occasionally until the porridge is cooked. It will be ready in about 20 minutes.

The proportions are $\frac{1}{2}$ lb of beremeal to 3 pints of water.

Beremeal Scones

Beremeal scones used to be made with beremeal porridge. Make the porridge as thick as possible—much thicker than for supping—season lightly with salt and add a good knob of butter.

Flour the baking board and turn the porridge out on to it. Leave it until it is cool enough to handle. Knead it lightly, then roll out in very thin rounds. Cut in triangles, and, keeping in rounds, bake on a hot girdle, first on one side and then on the other.

The scones should be eaten hot with butter.

Black Puddings (1)

Break the clots of some ox blood and run it through a sieve. Mix in some new, sweet milk according to the quantity of blood and season with black pepper and salt. The proportions are 1 pint of milk to 1 gallon of blood.

Shred suet finely and take half that quantity of oatmeal, mix well together and stir into the blood. Cut the skins, very clean, all to the same size and fill them slackly with the mixture, using a wide funnel. Tie at both ends.

Put them into a roomy pan three quarters full of water almost at boiling point. Bring slowly to boiling point and after 15 minutes prick them with a knitting kneedle. Boil for 2 hours, seeing that the water does not boil in.

To reheat, boil them gently in water for 15 minutes and finish on a brander in front of the fire.

Black Puddings (2)

Procure some pig's blood and at once salt it and strain it. Mix in a pint of new milk to every gallon of blood and thicken with finely minced suet and toasted oatmeal. Season with pepper and salt. Fill prepared skins, pin up the ends and boil gently for 2 hours.

Cool and store. To serve, reheat gently and birstle in front of the fire.

Beestings

For three days after calving the liquid a cow gives is not the milk we know, but colostrum, often called beestings. It has a very high protein content and contains globulin which gives it a solidifying quality when very gently heated, but which makes it lumpy if brought to the boil. This is known as 'new cheese', 'calfie's cheese' or 'beestie cheese' according to the locality.

Beestie Cheese

The second milking of a newly calved cow is the best for making beestie cheese. Flavour sufficient milk from this milking according to taste with sugar, and the merest 'fing'r an' thum' ' of salt. Throw in a spoonful of carvies (caraway seeds) *or* sultanas and put into the oven goblet. Snug the pot among the peats at the side of the fire, making sure the lid is tight, top it with quaillies (live peats) and leave it all afternoon.

This is one of the old Scots recipes using an oven pot, but it was quite often baked in a pie dish in an ordinary oven. It was hawked round the villages where there was a ready sale.

Breakfast Patty

A clove of garlic
A slice of onion
4 oz bacon fat

$\frac{1}{2}$ lb sliced calf's liver
$\frac{1}{2}$ lb (boneless weight) sliced veal
Pepper and *perhaps* salt

Parboil the onion for 3 minutes. Put a little of the bacon fat into a saucepan after rubbing it well with the garlic. Melt the fat and lightly fry (without browning) the onion, then the liver and the veal. Add a cupful of hot water, a suspicion of ground mace and a dust of grated nutmeg.

Let the meat cook until tender and leave it to cool in the liquor. Go over it carefully for fibres and then pound the two in the mortar until absolutely smooth. Reduce the liquor to about a tablespoonful, melt the rest of the bacon fat in it and strain it.

Begin to work this into the paste and when it is all in taste it and see if it requires more seasoning; the bacon fat may have enough salt for the paste. Work into pots keeping very smooth and cover with clarified butter sealing perfectly with the rim of the pot.

Knotty Tams

Allow 1 cupful of milk and 1 oz of oatmeal per person with a nieve-ful of meal to the bargain (that is as much oatmeal as you can lift with the hand), a spare cup of milk, and syrup and salt to taste.

Bring the milk to the boil, stir in the oatmeal and bring to the boil again over a low heat in case it 'scaums' (scorches), for 20 minutes. Season now to taste with a pinch of salt and about a spoonful of syrup. Add the spare cup of milk and bring to the boil again, take from the heat and at once drop in your handful of meal; mix a very little with a spoon but on no account stir it.

This dish is also made with 'beestings' (the milk of a newly calved cow) in some parts of Scotland. The second or third milking is preferred as the first milking is very deep in colour and not very appetising.

Crowdie (Cream)

Crowdie is made with sour milk or sweet milk and rennet. If you have milk that is just on the turn leave it a good 12 hours. Then heat it just enough and no more to separate the curd from the whey. On no account make it hot as this toughens the curd. Pour it into a piece of muslin and leave it to drain. The whey can be used for drinking.

When the whey is completely drained off, turn the crowdie into a bowl, mix it well, breaking down the curd until it is very fine. Season with salt and it is ready to eat. To make this a royal dish add as much thick cream as it will take.

Serve with oatcakes, lettuce and a glass of milk. Favourite flavourings used to be caraway seed, finely chopped chives or both and, without either, celery salt.

Crowdie with Sweet Milk

To make crowdie with sweet milk, set the required amount of milk warm from the cow with a dessertspoonful of rennet to each pint of milk. If you do not have your own cow, heat the milk to blood heat before adding to the rennet.

Let it sit a full 12 hours then break the curd with a fork and proceed as if for sour milk.

Junket: Yirned Milk

To make junket for the table use 1 teaspoonful of rennet to 1 pint of milk fresh from the cow or milk heated to blood heat. Set in individual bowls and serve with cream and oatcakes.

Curds and Cream: Mima's

Melt 1 teaspoonful of fine sugar in 2 teaspoonfuls of sherry in individual dishes. Heat the milk to blood heat and add a large teaspoonful of rennet to each pint of milk. Pour at once over the sherry, stir just a little and leave to set.

When quite firm add a blob of whipped cream.

Rennet

Rennet is the agent used to set, coagulate or yirn sweet milk and is prepared from the inner membrane of a calf's fourth stomach, called the vell. Before commercial rennet came on the market, a piece of this membrane was kept in most kitchen cupboards and dairies. It could be washed and dried and used many times. My own mother used a piece of this to make rennet and referred to it as 'the bittie skin'. It was kept in a muslin bag and from time to time was infused in a little water.

The fresh milk was set with this infusion and left in the dairy. Just before it was taken to the table a blanket of cream was lifted with a perforated skimmer from a pan of milk and slid on to the yirned milk. Oatcakes were always served with it. The hedgerow plant, Lady's Bedstraw is often called Rennet in the Highlands, but I have no knowledge of it being used as rennet.

The lining of turkey gizzards was also used and esteemed as rennet, known as gallino.

Cheese Pudding (1898)

Parboil an onion then slice it and gently infuse it in a pint of milk along with a spray of parsley. Cut a fairly thick slice of bread, remove the crusts, butter it and then spread a little mustard on it. Cut into cubes and fit neatly as a base to a greased pudding dish, buttered side down. Cover with very finely grated cheese and dust lightly with black pepper.

Beat two eggs, season with salt and pour the infused milk through a strainer on to the eggs, beating well. Pour over the cheese. Bake in a slow oven until firmly set and brown with a salamander or under the grill.

Cheese on Toast: Colonel Cameron's Recipe

2 oz butter	Shake of cayenne pepper and
6 oz grated Chedder cheese	black pepper
1 saltspoonful salt	2 tablespoonfuls thin cream
1 small teaspoonful made	4 slices of bread
mustard	2 pickled gherkins

Chop the gherkins into small pieces and warm them in a saucepan. Cream the butter with the seasoning, slowly work in the cream and then the grated cheese. Trim the crusts off the bread and toast on one side only.

Spread the cheese mixture on the untoasted sides of the bread and toast under the grill at a rather gentle heat until the mixture bubbles and turns a golden brown. Top with the warmed gherkins and serve at once.

Mrs Glennie's Potted Tongue (1885)

Cook one ox tongue long and slowly in a pot deep enough to allow it to be quite covered with water. Add a small piece of salt bacon, a dozen peppercorns, a blade of mace, a handful of shallots, 2 bay leaves and 6 cloves. It will take several hours to cook. Skim the water from time to time to remove impurities which may cloud the flavour. *Do not add salt.*

When the tongue is really tender take it from the fire. When it is cool enough to handle remove the skin and all pieces that may be tough or fibrous and slice the meat. Put it through the mincer with the finest blade then pound it in a morter until it is very smooth. Now taste it. If salt is required add it now, but lightly, and a few grains of cayenne. Then start to work in 6 oz of butter just melted and no more. It must be very smooth and of a delicate flavour; nothing should overpower the taste of the tongue itself. Work into small potting pots, pressing firmly so as not to leave air spaces.

When absolutely cold cover the top of each pot with clarified butter running it well to the edges of the pot so that you have a seal with the rim of the pot. This paté keeps a long time in a cool storeroom, particularly if you did have a piece of salted bacon to boil with it.

Miss Minnie's Omelette (for two)

An omelette should be light and moist and a really good one has pockets of egg that is just set and no more—slobbery, you might say. Do not beat it a lot or cook it in a big frying pan. But do use butter or bacon fat.

It is nonsense to say that an omelette pan should never be washed: the pan should be very clean and dry. Heat a good knob of butter or a spoonful of bacon fat in the pan. When ready for the omelette it should be at the sizzling stage but not turning brown.

With the pan on a medium heat, two plates heating and the other diner tethered to the table, break four eggs into a bowl. Add a little pepper and salt and 1 tablespoonful of milk or cream, and with a knife beat quickly while you count to thirty.

Drop the mixture into the sizzling fat, and give it a stir just as if you were making scrambled eggs. The underside begins to set and with a knife or a fork lift the omelette all round the edge and let the runny part go under until all the egg is set and no more. Tilt the pan if necessary.

Then tip the pan towards you, a sort of downward movement, and the omelette will slide half way up the rim of the pan. With the knife or fork fold it over, divide it in two, dish on the hot plates and eat at once.

Bacon, mushrooms, kidneys, onions, tomatoes, cheese, or two or three of them together all go well with omelette in their different ways, but all must be prepared, and cooked *before* you start to make the omelette.

A quick rub with a piece of butter glazes an omelette.

Ena Dodd's Cheese 'Crab' (1906)

4 oz finely grated cheese	½ teaspoonful salt
1 tablespoonful vinegar	1 hard boiled egg
1 tablespoonful butter	White pepper and cayenne
½ teaspoonful sifted sugar	

Hard boil the egg and while still warm put it through a wire sieve. Grate the cheese finely and oil the butter but on no account cook it. Put the egg and cheese into a bowl, add the seasoning and the butter and begin working the mixture to the smoothness of paste, adding the vinegar as you work. (*Note: Taste and make sure that all this vinegar will be tolerated. It may be too much.*)

Pack it into small pots and cover with paper dipped in brandy or white of egg (do not use clarified butter).

Boiled Potatoes

The cooking of potatoes can make or marr them and there is nothing finer than a well-cooked potato.

If they are to be boiled in their skins they should be well washed in luke-warm water and lightly scrubbed with a brush. Make a slit all the way round the middle of each potato. Boil them briskly in salted water, just covering them, for 20 minutes, then try them with a fork. If soft all the way through pour off the water, replace the lid and let them sit in their own steam for a little, giving them a vigorous shake from time to time.

Peeled potatoes are cooked in the same way and by taking them just before they are fully boiled and allowing them to cook in their own steam, you get the full flavour of the potato.

New potatoes should be cooked in boiling water: old potatoes which look a little tired can be much improved by leaving for some hours in a bowl of cold water.

To make a really good job of mashed potatoes heat a little milk with a knob of butter in it and add to the potatoes.

Stovies or Stoved Potatoes

The traditional stovies were made with potatoes, some fat and a little water and were served with oatcakes and a bowl of milk. Today stovies are often made with scraps of left-over meat and onions added to the potatoes.

Allow 3 good-sized potatoes and 1 onion per person. Slice the onions. Peel and slice the potatoes. Heat some good fat into a stew pan (gourmets say it must be an iron pan). Fry the onion in it first, then put in the sliced potatoes and season well with pepper, salt and some celery salt. Let them cook gently with the lid on stirring them from time to time. If you find the mixture a little dry add a cupful of boiling water.

Do not worry if they brown a little in the bottom of the pan as birstled stovies are delicious.

Oven Stovies

Wash and peel the required number of potatoes, and slice them fairly thickly. Slice an onion and parboil it if you find onion indigestible. Grease a roasting tin or a large pudding dish and arrange the potatoes in it, dusting them with pepper and salt. Cover with the sliced onion and add a cupful of milk or cream. Heat gently until the potatoes are cooked.

Serve with oatcakes and a glass of milk.

Hairst Stovies

For hungry men think in terms of half a stone of potatoes, a pound of cheese and several large onions. For a domestic dish allow 1 large onion and 2 oz of grated cheese to four potatoes. Pare and slice the potatoes and the onion. Heat a spoonful of dripping in a strong saucepan and fill in the ingredients, first a layer of onion, then a layer of cheese, and over that a layer of potatoes until they are all used up. Season each layer with pepper and salt.

Put the lid on and place the pan on heat sufficient to cook slowly for anything from $1\frac{1}{2}$ to 2 hours, depending on the quantity you use. This should cook in its own steam but do not hesitate to add a cupful of hot water if necessary.

Served with sweet milk and oatcakes, they are eaten with a spoon.

Bacon Stovies

4 oz lean bacon or gammon	Chopped parsley
2 lb potatoes	Pepper
2 large onions	

Peel the potatoes and cut them into chunky pieces. Peel and par-boil the onions and then slice them. Cut the bacon into small pieces. Heat some good fat or butter in a stewpan. Fry the onion lightly, then add the bacon and fry it. Then add the prepared potatoes.

Season with pepper, but do not add salt until the stovies are cooked, by which time you can taste and decide. Pour in a good cupful of water, bring to the boil and put the lid on.

Cook gently until the potatoes are ready, sprinkle with the parsley and serve with a glass of milk and oatcakes.

Marrow Bones: Sandy's

Buy a large beef leg of bone from your butcher and get him to saw it into lengths to suit your taste. Give the marrow at both ends of the bone the merest dust of pepper and salt and wrap each bone in a firm dough made with flour and water making sure they are sealed.

Lay side by side on a pudding cloth lined with greaseproof paper, tie firmly and place them in a fish kettle with boiling water to cover them.

Boil for an hour and then lift the strainer and let the bundle drip. Undo it with caution, carefully remove the hap from the bones and set each bone on a round of toast.

Serve at once with a small spoon.

Fritters

The present day dinette in a corner of the kitchen would perhaps have pleased Miss Minnie who had ideas on the subject of fritters. She says: 'Fritters can only be a success where punctuality is a virtue; they can only reach perfection when put from the pan to the plate.'

Batter

4 oz flour	1 dessertspoonful salad oil
2 eggs	1 dessertspoonful brandy
1 gill milk	

Put the flour into a basin which allows for beating. Add the yolks of the eggs and a little of the milk and mix to a cream. Beat steadily, adding the oil and brandy slowly and then the rest of the milk. Beating is more effective when the mixture is not too thin so do not add the last of the milk until the end of the beating. Beat for about 10 minutes in all and then set aside for at least an hour. When about to use add the whites of the 2 eggs beaten fairly stiff, folding them in rather than beating.

Have a pan of cooking fat, lard, or oil at just under boiling point (the temperature of the fat is of great importance; if it is too hot it will burn the fritters, if not hot enough, they will be soft). The fat should be just beginning to give off a very faint blue smoke and it can be tested by a spoonful of the batter. It should fluff up at once and colour a pale golden brown slowly.

This batter can be fried in spoonfuls then rolled in fine sugar and served as a sweet. It can also be used to coat fish, raw or cooked, slivers of cooked fowl, game or slices of hardboiled eggs. It can be used to make banana, pineapple or apple fritters and to coat small patties of a cheese mixture to serve as a savoury. For the latter, the addition of mustard gives a bite to the savoury.

Gruel

Soak a tablespoonful of oatmeal in a cupful of cold water. Let it sit for a couple of hours and then put it through a fine sieve.

Bring a cupful of milk to the boil, and pour it over the mealy liquid, stirring well: then return the whole to the pan.

Bring it to the boil, stirring all the time as it singes very readily. Let it cook for 5 minutes then season to taste with salt, sugar or honey. It can also be laced with whisky or rum.

The Haggis

There are many different ways of making a haggis as far as the composition of the materials are concerned. Some people like minced tripe in it, some do not; some only like a very small portion of the lights. This recipe, however, is a standard one and, for those who take the trouble to make it, it will indeed be rewarding.

Procure the large stomach bag of a sheep, also one of the smaller bags called the king's hood, together with the 'pluck' which is the lights, the liver and the heart. The bags take a great deal of washing. They must be washed first in flauchts of cold water, then plunged in boiling water and after that they must be scraped. Take great care of the bag which is to be filled for if it is damaged it is useless. After you are satisfied that it is as clean as you can make it let it lie in cold salted water overnight. The pluck must also be thoroughly well washed; you cook it along with the little bag.

Boil the pluck and the little bag in a big goblet with plenty of water (leaving the windpipe hanging over the side of the goblet as this allows impurities to pass out freely) for about an hour and a half before removing it from the goblet and allowing it to cool.

When cold, start preparing the filling by cutting away the windpipe and any gristle and skin. Use only a third of the liver and grate it, then mince the heart, the lights and the small bag. It may well be that you find that the heart and the king's hood are not boiled enough in the hour and a half, and if this is so put them back into the liquor and boil until tender.

Chop finely ½ lb of beef suet.

Toast three handfuls of oatmeal in front of the fire and then mix all the ingredients—minced lights, grated liver, minced heart, king's hood, suet, oatmeal, salt and a good shaking of black pepper and a saltspoonful of Jamaica pepper. Make this into a soft consistency with the liquor in which the pluck etc. was boiled; then fill into the stomach bag. Fill only a little over half full as the mixture swells. Sew up the bag with strong thread and the haggis is now ready for cooking.

Have a goblet which will hold it easily already on the fire with water almost at boiling point. Put in the haggis and bring the water to the boil. Keep it boiling steadily for 3 hours, pricking occasionally with a darning needle to allow air to escape. It is advisable to have a plate in the pan.

The haggis should be served on a napkin on an ashet without garnish or sauce.

A Simple Haggis

½ lb liver in a piece	4 oz chopped suet
½ lb cooked tripe	4 oz chopped onion
4 oz fine oatmeal	Salt and black pepper

Boil the liver in a saucepan with just enough water to cover it for 15 minutes (this is just long enough to 'set' it). Grate it or put it through the mincer; mince the cooked tripe also.

Mix all the ingredients, seasoning well with the pepper and salt. Make it into a moist dough with some of the liquor in which the liver was cooked. Boil in a pudding cloth for 2 hours or steam in a bowl for 3 hours.

Tomato Sandwiches: Murraybank

Peel the required number of tomatoes, and slice them thinly on to a broad ashet. Dust them heavily with pepper, salt and fine sugar. Take a chunky piece of brown bread and rub it through a fine wire sieve over the tomatoes, dust this with pepper and a very little salt and cover with a plate. Leave until the crumbs soak up all the juice.

Butter some brown bread, cut not too thinly, spread with the tomato mixture, put another slice on top and eat at once.

Roes in 'Egg' Cups

Hard-boil the required number of eggs and let them get quite cold. Cook some herring roes in boiling salted water for a few minutes, then drain them. Break them up and toss in butter. Cut the eggs in half, remove the yolk which should be finely sieved on to the roes, and season with pepper, salt and a pinch of powdered mace. Mix but do not mush.

Coat the 'cups' with beaten egg and crumb. Fry them in a basket in hot fat for a few minutes. Fill with the mixture and serve on toast at once.

Eggs in Gaelic

I was once shown by a cook how this dish was made but she shook her head over the name of it. 'It's the pity you haven't the Gaelic', she said. She did, however, write down the name and a friend translated it as 'Nun's Beads': I am assured there is such a dish which has cheese in it. Although there is no cheese in this recipe one might well use cheese instead of fish.

4 hardboiled eggs	1 oz butter
4 oz fillet of yellow haddock	1½ oz plain white flour
½ pint milk	1 teaspoonful anchovy essence

Cook the fillet in the milk and then pound it until very fine. Measure the milk and if it has boiled in make it up to the ½ pint. Melt the butter in a saucepan, mix in the flour and then slowly add the fish milk until the sauce is smooth. Bring to the boil and add the anchovy essence which is meant more as a colouring than a flavouring; but, if you like it, add more. Taste now to see if salt is necessary: this is most unlikely. Add the fish, pour out on to a plate and allow it to get quite cold.

Shell the eggs, and dip them in flour. Beat an egg well and put some very fine oatmeal into a bowl. Take a spoonful of the mixture and coat the hard-boiled eggs evenly. Drop the coated eggs into the beaten egg and then, one at a time, drop them into the oatmeal. Rotate the bowl until each egg is heavily coated and then fry in deep fat, not too hot, until the eggs are a golden brown.

Have some hot creamed potato ready, make a nest for each egg and serve hot.

If you use ordinary white fish you will, of course, require salt. If salmon, cook it in water and omit the essence. If cheese, use 2 oz grated cheese and 2 oz flour, a little mustard, pepper and salt, and essence if you like it.

Carrot and Turnip

These are root vegetables and are 'married' from long association, many recipes saying 'add carrot and turnip'. Both lend sweetness as well as other flavours to soups and stews: indeed, they are indispensable in many soups. If boiled separately to be added to some dish or to serve as a vegetable with meat, keep the liquor in which they were cooked; it is very useful to add to soups, such as lentil, split pea or potato.

Dried Vegetables

Peas, beans, barley and even lentils should be well steeped in cold water. If split peas or whole green peas are particularly stubborn when it comes to cooking, steeping in boiling water is a great help.

Green Vegetables

Green vegetables, such as sprouts, kail or cabbage which have become a little wilted, can be much revived with a long drink of cold water.

Boiling Whole Rice

Perhaps more has been said about the correct way to boil rice than about all the other vegetables put together. Old time cooks set great store by this accomplishment and many a kitchenmaid won or lost a 'situation' on this score. Almost every cook had her own secret about it; there were recipes called 'The Black Man Cooks Rice' and 'The Chinese Chef's Recipe', the method used on one of the famous liners of earlier days was given in a fashionable paper; I found one among Colonel Cameron's recipes, all of which are excellent.

Rice can absorb four times its own weight in liquid and, to be really successfully cooked, should boil evenly and steadily for half of the time; the other half it should cook in its own steam.

Allow 1 oz per person. Wash it well. Have plenty of water in a saucepan, add salt and some lemon juice to it. Bring to the boil and add the rice. Let it boil with the rice moving freely for 15 minutes. Test it: it should have a 'bone' in it—a hard minute piece of core.

Pour the rice into a colander and then wash under the cold tap. Set the colander into the pan, cover with a clean towel and return to the stove. It will take 10 minutes thus to remove that core. Or line a pie dish with buttered paper, put the rice in it, tuck paper over and leave in a warm corner such as the rack over the stove or coolish part of the oven.

If you wish to use the rice stock set the colander into a basin and retain the liquid.

Seakale

Seakale is cooked like asparagus. It has a very delicate flavour and care must be taken to preserve it. Wash the stalks well, cut them into even lengths and tie in bundles. Drop them into a pan of boiling salted water with a few drops of lemon juice in it. Cook until tender. It may take 30 minutes but test after 20 minutes.

Serve it on toast, keeping the heads all one way. Butter sauce, melted butter or white sauce may be served with it.

Scotch Kale

Scotch kale or curly greens are cooked like any other greens—in boiling salted water. Strip them off the coarser part of the stalk and wash well in salty water.

To serve, strain well, add a little butter and a cupful of cream and mash.

The Onion Family

This is a bulb vegetable and is one of our more important vegetables. They have a high food value and give flavour and savour to our food.

Onions

In Britain we perhaps know the onion best but leeks, garlic, chives shallots are all in the same group. A well dried onion has a fine papery skin which should be removed. As many find onions indigestible, parboiling them—dropping them into boiling water and letting them cook in it for 5 minutes—will take away some of the volatile oil which causes the trouble. After parboiling they can be cooked in many ways—fried, stuffed, or for flavouring stews and ragouts.

Leeks

The leek is one of the blanched vegetables and was said to be a beautifier and a blood purifier. The green part should be firm, and the white part very white. Care must be taken in washing them as they can harbour earth or sand between the layers.

Porridge

The proportions for a good porridge are 2 oz of oatmeal to 1 pint of water. As an old cookery book has it, 'a guid nievefu' and a bittock oatmeal' to a pint of water. (As a matter of fact the average hand can lift 1½ oz of oatmeal at a time.)

Bring the water to the boil and, with the oatmeal in one hand and a wooden spoon or spurtle in the other, stir in the oatmeal. Sprinkle it in slowly and go on stirring until the mixture thickens a little, add ½ a teaspoonful of salt, then lower the heat and let the porridge cook gently for 30 minutes.

You can soak oatmeal or rolled oats in a little cold water and leave overnight: this of course reduces the cooking time and the risk of 'knots'.

Risotto

1 onion	4 oz grated cheese
4 oz whole rice	1 oz butter
1 pint stock (preferably chicken)	Pepper, salt and made mustard
6 medium-sized tomatoes	

Wash the rice and let it drain well. Melt half of the butter in a saucepan and fry the rice in it before adding the onion finely chopped. Pour in the stock, add the seasoning and bring to the boil. Set over a very low heat and let it cook until all the stock is absorbed.

Peel the tomatoes by dropping them in boiling water for a minute, removing the skins, and slice them thickly. Fry them in the rest of the butter and season them with pepper and salt and a few grains of sugar. Lay them on the top of the cooked rice and then add the grated cheese. Stir lightly through the rice without making it mushy.

Serve very hot.

Miss Mary's Risotto

1 teacupful whole rice
1 large onion
2 breakfastcupfuls stock
(chicken for preference)

2 heaped tablespoonfuls grated
cheese
Pepper, salt, and a saltspoonful
mustard
A few strands saffron

Infuse the stock with the saffron. Parboil the onion and cut it into very thin slices. Wash the rice and leave it to drain. Bring a piece of butter in a saucepan to sizzling point and fry the onion in it until it is a pale golden brown: then fry the rice.

Strain the stock over it, season with pepper and salt and the mustard mixed with some of the stock. Bring to the boil, stirring until it does boil to prevent it sticking. Set it to a cooler part of the stove and let it sit just under cooking point until the rice has absorbed the stock. It will take at least 30 minutes.

Just before serving, fold in the grated cheese. Serve very hot with snippets of toast.

Mealie Crashie

2 oz good dripping
½ lb oatmeal

½ cup boiling water

This can be made with the fat in the frying pan after frying bacon or sausages or with dripping. Fry the oatmeal in the hot fat for a few minutes: season with pepper and salt if necessary. Add the boiling water and cook, stirring all the time, until the oatmeal comes cleanly away from the sides of the pan.

Skirlie

Melt an ounce of shredded suet, beef or mutton, in a frying pan. Slice an onion—more if you like—and stir until it is cooked but not browned. Now stir in two handfuls of oatmeal, add a little salt, a good shake of pepper and another ounce of chopped suet. Keep turning the skirlie in the pan until the meal takes on a golden tint.

Serve very hot.

Steamed Mealy Pudding

½ lb medium oatmeal
¼ lb finely shredded suet
1 onion

Pepper and salt
A saltspoonful of bicarbonate
of soda

Parboil and chop the onion. Mix all the ingredients to a dropping consistency with milk, water or stock from boiled beef. Put into a greased bowl, cover with greased paper and a cloth and steam steadily for 1½ hours.

(Parboiling an onion for this kind of dish does away with all risk of the onion not cooking in the given time.)

Emily's Scotch Eggs

Take ¾ lb of cold minced chicken or veal with a little cooked ham or a mixture of all three. Season to taste and add a suspicion of rosemary.

Make a sauce with:

½ oz plain white flour
½ pint milk
2 oz butter

Pepper, salt and again the merest
hint of rosemary

Add the meat to the sauce and allow to cool. Hard boil the eggs, shell them, dry them in flour then cover smoothly with the mixture so that there is no fear of cracks. Coat with beaten egg, rotate in a bowl of dried breadcrumbs and fry in deep fat until golden brown.

Cut in half and set the point of each egg in a nest of creamed potatoes and arrange in a circle on a hot dish. Fill in the centre with buttered tiny peas and cubes of carrot. Top with a bunch of parsley, crisp and green, or fried.

Sowens

Sowens were made with the flour of oatmeal that lurked in the inner husks ('sids') of the oat grain. The interesting thing about the making of sowens is that a complete kit of utensils was used for this and nothing else. These were a small wooden tub (or bowie), a hair search, a sowen's sieve, and a large earthenware jar.

The sids were obtained from the meal mill and were soaked in cold water in the tub. They were left in the tub until they became slightly sour; in cold weather it might take as long as a fortnight, in summer about four days would be sufficient. A stir each day helped to shake down the flour.

The sowen's sieve is a small wooden trough with a perforated bottom of white iron and two pieces of wood to form handles. This is set in a clean milk basin and the sids lifted into it, and pressed down. The hair sieve is put over the earthenware crock and the liquid poured through the sieve into the crock. Let this sit overnight so that the flour can settle and then much of the water can be poured off.

To cook, fresh water is added to so much of the solid. At this stage they are known as raw sowens. The mixture is then boiled. The thickness depends on the meal: if for supping, they are the texture of a gruel; if for drinking, much thinner.

Syrup, honey, cream, and butter were served with sowens according to taste.

(The Scot and oatmeal have always been bracketed together but in Markham's 'English Housewife, 1653', a food called wash-bree is described as being made with small oatmeal long steeped then boiled to a jelly and eaten with wine, whey, honey or ale according to taste.)

Madame's Eggs en Cocotte

This is a most delightful recipe with endless scope for variety and can also be presented in the most attractive way. Madame kept china dishes which were used for nothing else, and I have used small marmite pots or even teacups to cook them. The important point is that the cups must be deep without being broad: a small tea cup is the best indication of size I can give.

Heavily butter the cups according to the number required. Break an egg, drop the white into the cup and the yolk into another bowl. There are an almost endless variety of fillings which can be added, but a simple example is very finely grated Gouda cheese dusted with pepper.

Beat the yolks, add a little salt and a suspicion of made mustard and then work the cheese into the yolk. Take a heaped teaspoonful of the mixture and put it lightly into the white. You will see now why you need deepish narrow dishes as the mixture should be quite covered with white when cooked.

Cover the pots and steam for 10 minutes. Again you will understand the filling must be something very easily cooked or already cooked. Longer steaming will toughen the white.

The eggs can be served hot or cold but must in either case be turned out of the cup. They can be topped with something colourful like grated carrot and surrounded with cooked sprigs of cauliflower which have been tossed in butter and sprinkled with chopped parsley. I find young green peas or tiny beans glistening with butter add greatly to the appearance of a dish. You can lightly cut the top of the egg in a cross and turn back the points to reveal the filling and put a sprig of parsley or a scrap of watercress on top.

You may find you have more yolk than you can use: if so steam them until hard in a little salted water and rub through a sieve over the eggs.

Savoury Pancakes

4 oz fine oatmeal
2 oz plain white flour
1 egg

½ teaspoonful of baking powder
Saltspoonful of salt
Milk

Soak the oatmeal for some hours, or even overnight, in a little milk. Beat the egg well, and sift the flour with the salt and baking powder. Add all this to the oatmeal and add sufficient milk to make a pouring consistency. Fry in spoonfuls in hot fat. They are very good when fried in the pan after bacon has been cooked, but if so, do not add salt to the mixture.

Tomatoes in a Dressing (to serve with lettuce)

Take the required number of tomatoes and blanch them for a second in a pan of boiling water, then take off a very thin skin. Slice the tomatoes thinly into a wide shallow bowl.

Then put a small teaspoonful of made mustard into a bowl and add some salt, pepper and a few grains of castor sugar. Stir in 3 tablespoonfuls of salad oil, and 1 tablespoonful of vinegar or lemon juice. Mix well and pour over the tomatoes.

Sprinkle some finely chopped chives and a little chopped parsley over them and allow to mellow for an hour.

Devilled Almonds

Blanch, peel and dry ½ lb of Jordan almonds; heat 6 oz of butter not too hot, and add 1½ tablespoonfuls of salt, a shake of cayenne, black pepper, paprika, and castor sugar. Shake nuts in this until crisp and brown.

Eggs

It is taken for granted that everybody knows how to cook an egg but much depends on how you like your egg done. The correct way is a firm yet tender white and a creamy yolk; and the best method to achieve this is to boil the egg in some slightly salted, rapidly boiling water for 1 minute; then set the pan back from the heat and let it sit for 5 minutes. The most commonly used way is to put the egg into sharply boiling water, boil for 4 minutes and remove at once from the water.

Hard-boiled Eggs

Again have the water at the boil and boil the eggs steadily for 15 minutes. Remove them at once from the water and plunge into very cold water. If not for immediate use gently free the shell from the egg *without* removing it and keep in cold water. Shelled eggs toughen when not covered. Putting eggs on in cold water to hard boil may result in a dark line round the yolk.

The salt in the water when boiling eggs may prevent a crack from becoming a 'bust'.

Oatmeal Stuffing for Boiled Fowl

$\frac{1}{2}$ lb medium oatmeal $\frac{1}{4}$ lb onion
$\frac{1}{4}$ lb suet   Pepper and salt

Chop the suet. Parboil the onion and chop it up very small. Mix all the ingredients together and work them into a ball. (Very useful for stuffing fish, and for vegetables such as onions and cabbage.)

To make a Devil

Put an ounce of butter into a mortar and work in:

$\frac{1}{2}$ teaspoonful salt   Snifter of paprika
1 teaspoonful made mustard   Snifter of ground mace
1 teaspoonful sharp sauce   Snifter of black pepper
Snifter of cayenne

A Devil for Turkey Legs

1 clove of garlic or some shallot finely chopped
½ teacupful tarragon vinegar
3 cupfuls good turkey stock
1 oz butter
1 oz flour

12 peppercorns
Salt, mustard, black pepper
Worcester sauce
A dessertspoonful hot chutney
A few drops Tabasco
Chopped parsley

Put the stock, vinegar, clove of garlic or shallot and the peppercorns into a pan and bring to the boil. Let this infuse for about half an hour, and reduce in boiling. Strain it and let it cool.

Melt the butter in a sauce pan, add the flour and then the devilled stock and cook to a smooth sauce. Add all the other seasoning and taste. Add more if you think the balance of flavour is not just right.

Score the turkey drumsticks and other parts of brown turkey meat and soak for an hour in the sauce. Drain them well, grill them under a hot grill and serve with the sauce. (A Devil is very much a matter of personal taste and the above recipe is merely a good guide, to which many cooks will add.)

Herb Stuffing (for fish, poultry or pork)

2 cupfuls fine white breadcrumbs
1 dessertspoonful finely chopped onion
1 dessertspoonful finely chopped parsley

½ teaspoonful mixed herbs
Pepper, salt and paprika
A spoonful warm water or stock
2 oz melted butter

Apricot Stuffing for Pork

2 cupfuls dried apricots
1 orange
1 lemon
½ cup butter

4 cupfuls finely grated breadcrumbs
½ cupful walnuts
Pepper, salt and a pinch of ground mace

Soak the apricots in just enough boiling water to cover them and leave them for 12 hours. Cook, strain and mash, then add the grated rind of the orange and lemon and the juice of both. Stir in the breadcrumbs, add the butter melted and season. *Do not use any of the apricot juice as this would make the stuffing too soft.*

Rabbit Paté: Colonel Cameron's Recipe

2 lb raw rabbit flesh
1 lb raw veal
½ lb really good pork sausage-
    meat
Herbs and spices in powdered
    form

A wineglass of brandy
2 bay leaves, 2 sprigs thyme
Some shreds of sage
Salt
Slices of very very thin pork fat

Choose your rabbits with care: not too young but not too old. Wash them well and dry them, paying particular attention to the tail (*the minute piece of green membrane under the tail is the source of the so-called rabbity flavour.* See that not even a pinhead of it is left attached to the flesh.) With a sharp knife remove as much flesh as you require.

Cook the bones of the rabbits in water, salt, a few peppercorns, a suspicion of mace and an onion. Mince the rabbit flesh. Season lightly with salt, pepper, and the merest suspicion of spice.

Mince the veal and season it lightly. Keep it apart from the other ingredients.

Line the sides of a deep earthenware dish with the pork fat. On the bottom lay a bay leaf, a sprig of thyme and some sage. Cover with a base of sausagemeat, put in a layer of rabbit and then a layer of veal. Go on until all the rabbit and veal is in the dish, packing it tightly and keeping the fat lining in place. Finish with a layer of sausagemeat.

Pierce the paté from top to the very bottom many times with a sharp skewer. Take a cup of the rabbit stock now cold and add the brandy to it. Carefully fill this into the holes, letting it seep down and add more if it will take it. Cover with thin pork fat, a bay leaf, a sprig of thyme, sage, and put the lid on the dish. Seal the rim with a pastry dough. Cook in a moderate oven for 3 hours.

(The making of a paté requires perfection cooking and a cunning blend of flavouring, no one flavour predominating.)

Miss Maggie's Stuffing for Turkey

2 lb very lean pork
Turkey liver
5 large tablespoonfuls of fine
   white breadcrumbs

Pepper and salt
A finger-and-thumb of mixed
   herbs

Mince the pork twice. Drop the liver into a little boiling water in a saucepan and cook long enough to set it (about 15 minutes). Chop up the liver and add it to the pork and the breadcrumbs, season and add just enough of the liquor in which the liver was cooked to moisten the mixture.

Celery Stuffing (to go with Turkey)

Parboil the turkey liver and cut into tiny pieces. Parboil and chop finely 2 onions. Add a large cupful of finely chopped celery, a tablespoonful of chopped parsley, 5 oz of shredded suet, 8 oz of fine white breadcrumbs, a teaspoonful of mixed herbs, pepper, salt, 3 well beaten eggs and a spoonful of milk.

Mix into a firm mixture.

Chestnut Stuffing

1 lb chestnuts
1 lb sausagemeat
2 onions finely chopped
Some chopped parsley

A teaspoonful grated lemon rind
Pepper, salt
A saltspoonful grated nutmeg
1 egg

Shell, peel and roughly cut up the chestnuts. Add the seasoning to the egg and beat to a froth. Put the sausagemeat into the mixing bowl, add the other ingredients and bind with the egg.

Poacher's Partridge

Allow one bird per person and one to spare. Pluck, draw and truss the birds. Wash if necessary but it is better to wipe them out with damp cloth. Put the spare bird into a stock-pot with shallots, a blade of mace, pepper, salt, a few grains of sugar and some meat bones if possible and cover with cold water. Cook until the meat leaves the bones of the bird and put through a sieve.

Cut one large firm cabbage, soaked in salt water for an hour and then drained, in quarters and remove the core. Cook the four parts in salted water until part cooked and drain well, patting with a clean towel to remove surplus moisture.

Bring some good roast fat almost to boiling point in a deep saucepan. Lightly fry some slices of bacon, just enough to set them. Remove them and put in the birds, turning them until they are well browned all round. Take them out and put in flour, in the proportion of 1 oz flour to a pint of stock and gradually add the strained stock. Season with pepper and salt if necessary.

Line the pan now with the cabbage, lay the birds on top, and put the bacon on top of them. Dust with pepper. Put the lid on and cook gently until the birds are tender.

White Puddings

Have your skins all ready, thoroughly washed and cut in lengths. Toast the oatmeal. Take three times its weight in good suet very finely shredded and mix the meal and the suet, seasoning it well with black pepper and salt.

Fill the skins slackly using a wide funnel. Secure the ends with a wooden pin (or tie them with fine twine) and drop the puddings into a goblet of water just under boiling point. Bring gently to the boil and boil cannily for 2 hours. Jab occasionally with a fork to let air escape. Store when quite cold in the meal girnal or in a bin of bran.

To serve, heat in warm water then toast on the brander.

Bacon Pasties

This was one way of using the somewhat salty home-cured bacon of other days.

6 rashers bacon	Black pepper
4 good sized potatoes	Knob of butter
2 (or possibly more) tablespoon-fuls flour	

Peel and boil the potatoes without salt. Shake them dry and mash well. Put them into a baking bowl, add the butter and the pepper and gradually mix in the flour; work until quite smooth. Roll out on a well floured board and cut in six strips. Put a slice of bacon on each strip, fold over and press firmly, sealing all the edges. Bake in a moderate oven until pale golden brown and crisp. Time: about 30 minutes. A good smear of made mustard if you are a mustard addict on each slice of bacon.

A Cream Cheese, commonly called a Hangman (1750)

Wash well an ox or cow bladder in cold well water, then in several waters of lukewarm temperature. Fill it with cream: if there is not enough cream to fill the bladder tie it close by the cream so that there is no air below the tie.

Hang it up in the cellar for three weeks, in which time the cream will be earned by the bladder and the whey will filter and drop clear as water.

Turn the cheese out of the bladder in a lump; it will have the consistency of firm butter and the substance on the outside of the cheese will be softer than the rest and must be taken off with a knife or a spoon lest there be a trace of bitterness from contact with the bladder.

Thereafter you may mould it as you please. It needs no pressing and if you should desire it to become harder, dust the outside with fine salt and expose to the air for a few days.

Hatted Kit

You can make a hatted kit even if you do not have a cow but it is agreed that milk straight from the cow into the dish puts a better hat on the kit.

Heat to blood temperature 2 pints of buttermilk and add to it 3 teaspoonfuls of rennet. Pour it into a warm dish and take at once to the side of the cow. Quickly milk directly into the dish what you would take to be a pint of milk (a little over makes no difference but do not let it be under).

Take it back to the larder and allow to stand until it turns into curd. 'Coup' (empty) into a fine milk sey or strainer and shake until all the whey has run clear away. Put the curd into a bowl and season lightly with a little fine sugar and a grating of nutmeg. Beat some double cream and again season it with sugar and nutmeg and work into the curd.

If you do not have a cow a pint of milk at blood temperature will serve.

Note: Buy nutmegs that feel heavy for their size.

Baking

Self-raising Flour for Scones and Pancakes

Take 4 lb of plain white flour and add to it 2 oz of cream of tartar, 1 oz bicarbonate of soda and 1 teaspoonful salt. Mix this well on a large sheet of greaseproof paper and then put it through a fine sieve at least three times.

Keep in a dry container with a cover.

'Collaring' a Milk Pudding

A milk pudding can be enhanced by a collar of good shortcrust: put an attractive edging of paste on the pie dish, wetting the edge or rim of the dish before putting it on. Put a layer of a stiff jam such as apricot or pineapple in the bottom of the dish, pour in the milk pudding and bake in a moderate oven until the crust is brown.

It is also a useful method of using up odd scraps of pastry.

Barm Loaf

The barm loaf was baked in a pot with a strong iron lid. The pot was either hung over the peat fire with a burning peat on the lid, or it was snuggled down in a bed of glowing peat with a live peat on top.

1 lb fine oatmeal	A saltspoonful of salt and a
4 oz plain white flour	shake of pepper
1 teaspoonful bicarbonate of soda	1 tablespoonful treacle
	1 tablespoonful syrup
	Buttermilk

Sift the flour, bicarbonate of soda, salt and pepper into a baking bowl. Add the oatmeal and then trickle the syrup and treacle into it and mix to a soft dough with buttermilk so that it has an almost pouring consistency.

Pour into a well greased cake tin and bake in a moderate oven for 1 hour.

Morning Rolls (rowies, butteries) (1)

Sift 1 lb of plain white flour with 1 teaspoonful of salt into a warmed bowl, and rub in 3 oz of butter or margarine. Cream ½ oz of yeast with a few grains of sugar; or if *dried yeast,* use the quantity given on the tin for 1 lb of flour and melt it with not quite ½ a pint of hot water: this takes a little longer than compressed yeast, but is equally as good. The quantity of liquid is the same in both cases—not quite ½ pint of lukewarm water.

Make a stiff dough with the water and yeast, and knead until the dough is quite smooth. Spread it well over the bottom of the bowl so that it will be easily warmed all through. Cover with a damp towel and set in a warm place to rise until it has doubled in size.

Turn it out on to a well floured board and roll out as for pastry. Dot 1 oz of butter or margarine over the surface, fold in three, dust with flour and roll out. Repeat with another ounce of butter or margarine and fold again. Put it back into the bowl to recover from this handling and when it has risen again, handle it as little as possible, roll out and cut with a 3-inch cutter. Put on baking sheet. Prove in a warm place and bake until brown and crisp in a very hot oven (15 minutes).

Butteries (2)

Measure ¾ lb of flour into a warm bowl, add a good pinch of salt. Liquify ½ oz of dried yeast with 3 teaspoonfuls of sugar and just under ½ pint of water at blood temperature. Pour the yeast water into the flour and mix well; then knead into a smooth dough. Spread well over the bottom of the bowl, cover with a warm towel and set in a warm place to rise for about 30 minutes.

Cut 4 oz of lard, or lard and margarine mixed, into pieces and with a knife cut this through and through the risen dough. You now have a soft, fatty dough and you will require 4 oz of flour to knead and to make the dough into small lumps. Knead well, break into twelve pieces and if you are not good at judging size weigh each lump (they should be just about but not over 2½ oz). Round them nicely and put them on a warm baking sheet, well spaced, to prove, covered with a towel, in a warm place for another 30 minutes.

Bake in a moderately hot oven (about 400°F) until crisp and brown. Five minutes before taking them from the oven put a nut of butter on each roll.

White Baps

1 lb plain white flour
1 oz yeast
2½ oz lard

1 teaspoonful sugar
1 teaspoonful salt
½ pint of milk

Sift the flour with the salt into a warmed baking bowl and rub in the lard. Cream the yeast by rubbing it in a cup or small bowl with the sugar and then add it to the milk heated to blood temperature.

With this liquid make a soft dough and then leave it in a warm place, covered with a warm towel, until the dough doubles its size. Knead it lightly and divide it into small portions Shape into ovals and set on a warm floured baking sheet. Cover again with the warm towel and leave for 30 minutes to prove.

Dimple the centre of each bap with the thumb, dust liberally with flour and bake for 15 minutes at Gas 6 or 400°F.

Cloddie Broons (a kind of loaf)

1 lb plain white flour
4 oz butter or good dripping
6 oz soft brown sugar
4 oz currants
4 oz sultanas

1 teaspoonful each ground ginger, ground cinnamon and bicarbonate of soda
½ teaspoonful Jamaica pepper
A good pinch of salt
2 tablespoonfuls syrup
Buttermilk to mix

Rub the fat into the flour along with the sugar to act as a grater. Add all the other ingredients, and mix to a soft mixture with buttermilk. Turn into a well buttered loaf tin and bake in a moderate oven for 2½ hours.

Cookies

½ lb plain white flour	1 oz butter
½ oz yeast	½ teaspoonful of salt
1 teaspoonful castor sugar	1 gill milk

Rub the butter into the flour. Cream the yeast with the sugar, warm the milk to blood heat and add it to the yeast. With this mix the flour to a dough. Set to rise in a warm corner for about 1 hour until the yeast dough almost doubles its size. Knead well now, then divide into twelve portions. Shape into cookies and put on a greased tin. Leave to prove for 20 minutes.

Brush with a little milk in which castor sugar is dissolved and bake in a hot oven for 15 minutes.

Cream Buns

As above. Split the cookies and put beaten flavoured cream in them.

Bridie's Tea Rolls

½ lb plain white flour	1 level dessertspoonful sugar
½ teaspoonful baking powder	2½ oz butter
½ teaspoonful cream of tartar	Cold water to mix
¼ teaspoonful bicarbonate of soda	

Sift the dry ingredients together into a baking bowl and rub the butter in until the mixture is as fine as you can make it. Add sufficient water to make a paste, not quite as soft as a scone mixture but not as firm as for pastry. Knead it well on a floured board, working it into a square.

Roll it up, not too lightly, moisten the edges with water and with a very sharp knife cut into 1 inch thick slices. Bake in a very hot oven for 15 minutes. For an electric oven heat it to 500°F, and lower to 400°F when the rolls are put in.

Aul' Yule Cake

This is the black bun, a mixture of fruit, flour, nuts and spices baked in paste.

Paste

¾ lb plain white flour
½ teaspoonful baking powder
A good pinch of salt

5 oz of butter
Cold water to mix

Filling

1 lb plain white flour
1 teaspoonful bicarbonate of soda
1 large teaspoonful cream of tartar
½ oz ground cinnamon

½ oz ground ginger
¼ oz Jamaica pepper
A good shake of black pepper
A saltspoonful of ground nutmeg and the same of cloves

Sift all these at least three times.

2 lb blue raisins
2 lb currants
2 oz orange peel
2 oz lemon peel

2 oz citron peel
8 oz almonds
Milk to mix

First make a paste, keeping it fairly dry, roll it out evenly, and line a cake tin, keeping back sufficient to make a lid.

Stone the blue raisins and wash and pick over the currants, making sure they are quite dry before you use them. Choose whole peel and slice it thinly. Blanch and slice the almonds. Add all this to the flour, etc., and add enough milk to make a soft mixture. Pile into the lined tin keeping the top quite flat. Moisten the edges with cold water and fit on the lid which should be loose to allow the inside to rise a little. Take a long skewer and dab the cake in about six places, right to the bottom of the tin, then prick the top all over with a fork. Brush with a well beaten egg and bake in a moderate oven for 3½ hours.

Leave it in the tin for about 30 minutes before turning it out.

Albert Rock Cakes

½ lb plain white flour
1 teaspoonful baking powder
Pinch of salt
1 teaspoonful grated lemon rind
½ teaspoonful lemon essence

4 oz sultanas
3 oz butter
3 oz castor sugar
1 egg
2 tablespoonfuls milk

Sift the flour with the salt and baking powder and add the sugar. Rub in the butter; add the fruit and the lemon rind. Beat the egg well, add the milk to it and with this make a dough of the flour. The dough should be dry but it may take a little more milk. Put out in heaps on a greased baking sheet and bake in a slow oven for about 20 minutes until brown and crisp.

Brandy Creams

4 oz butter
2 oz lard
1 tablespoonful syrup
2 tablespoonfuls water
4 oz sugar

4 oz flour
4 oz porridge oats
1 teaspoonful bicarbonate of
  soda neither heaped nor level

Warm the butter, lard, syrup and water in a saucepan just sufficiently to melt the butter and lard. Add the rest of the ingredients and mix well. Put out in little balls on a well greased baking sheet, far apart, and bake in a slow oven until brown.

When cold put them together with:

4 oz butter
2 oz castor sugar
2 tablespoonfuls dried milk

2 tablespoonfuls warm water
½ teaspoonful vanilla essence

Beat the butter and sugar to a cream. Work in the dried milk and the water until you have a smooth cream. Flavour with the vanilla essence.

As an alternative filling, fresh cream beaten stiff, flavoured and slightly sweetened can be used. Essence of ginger with fresh cream makes a delightful filling.

A Chocolate Cake

3 oz plain white flour
3 eggs
4 oz castor sugar
2 oz butter

1 level teaspoonful baking
   powder
Pinch of salt

Line a cake tin with greased paper. Beat the eggs and the sugar until the mixture is light and foamy. It helps if you put the basin with the eggs and sugar into a bigger bowl filled with hot water.

Melt the butter and fold it in, then the flour sifted with the baking powder and the salt (fold in the flour rather than beat it in). Pour the mixture into the lined tin and bake in a moderate oven for about 30 minutes, a little longer if it feels soft to the touch.

When it is quite cold, cut it in three layers, and fill each layer with butter icing, then coat with chocolate icing.

Butter Icing

Sift 8 oz of icing sugar to make sure it is quite free from lumps. Soften 2 oz of butter a little in a bowl, add 1 teaspoonful of vanilla essence and gradually beat in as much of the sifted icing sugar as it will take without being stodgy.

As an alternative, use brandy instead of the essence.

Chocolate Icing

Sift $\frac{1}{2}$ lb of icing sugar and add 1 oz of cocoa to it. Mix it well. Melt an ounce of butter in 2 tablespoonfuls of milk a little warmer than lukewarm. Slowly add this to the icing sugar and cocoa and stir until quite smooth. Pour over the cake and spread with a knife.

Leave it at least 1 day to mellow.

Choux Pastry

This pastry is in a class by itself, different from any other pastry in method and in cooking, and is used mainly for eclairs and cream puffs. The standard rule for quantities is equal quantities of flour and water, half the weight of the flour in butter, and 3 eggs to every 4 oz of flour. Here are the quantities in both cups and ounces:

½ pint water	1 cup water
2 oz butter	1 cup flour
4 oz flour	½ cup melted butter
3 eggs *or*	3 eggs

Heat the water and the butter slowly to melt the butter evenly; then bring to the boil. Sift the flour and pour it as quickly as possible into the boiling water. Stir until it is smooth and creamy. Cook a little, stirring all the time till the paste leaves the sides of the pan, beating and mixing well. Remove it from the heat and let it cool, giving it an occasional stir. Now break an egg into it and beat it well; add the second egg and beat it well, then do the same with the third egg.

You should now have a smooth golden paste, velvety smooth, and just stiff enough to hold its shape on the spoon. You can now bake the paste in spoonfuls on a baking sheet, or in fingers, or you can fry it.

Cream Puffs

Grease a baking sheet and put the paste out on it in little spoonfuls, keeping them as round in shape as possible (about the size of a medium sized Brussels sprout). Brush them over lightly with a little well-beaten egg. If for eclairs, pipe them out with a forcing bag.

A hot oven of 450°F is needed for the first 10 minutes. After that lower to 375°F and cook in all for 30 minutes.

Filling the Puffs

When they are quite cold take a very sharp knife and cut off the tops. Fill with whatever filling you are going to use and replace the top. Savoury fillings, such as a little shredded fish in a good sauce, sweetbreads also in a sauce, creamed chicken are some suggestions, and of course, whipped cream sweetened and flavoured. If used as a sweet give them a light dust of icing sugar.

Chocolate Eclairs

Use the same paste. Pipe the paste out in fingers on a greased baking sheet and bake for 20 to 30 minutes. When cold, make a slit in each eclair, scoop out any soft centre there may be, fill with cream beaten and flavoured and finish with a chocolate icing.

French Crullers

These are fascinating to make. Make the choux pastry in the usual manner but add 1 dessertspoonful of castor sugar and a little grated lemon rind to the above quantities.

Pipe the paste out in rings on a sheet of greased paper cut to fit very easily into the frying basket and let them sit for a minute or two to firm up. Have a pan of frying fat or oil just at the faint blue smoking point and put in the frying basket.

Gently lower the paper, upside down, into the hot fat. In a minute the crullers will fall off the paper which can be lifted out and used for the next batch. Turn the crullers once or twice until they are a golden brown, then drain them on paper and toss in castor sugar.

Serve very hot.

A Christmas Cake

12 oz plain white flour	4 oz chopped mixed peel
10 oz butter	5 eggs
5 oz icing sugar	¼ teaspoonful ground mace
5 oz soft brown sugar	¼ teaspoonful ground Jamaica
8 oz currants	pepper
8 oz sultanas	½ teaspoonful ground cinnamon
8 oz blue raisins	¼ teaspoonful table salt
4 oz glace cherries	2 tablespoonfuls brandy

Line an 8-inch cake tin with grease proof paper. Set the oven at 500°F or Gas 8. Clean the fruit but leave the cherries whole. Sieve the two sugars into a roomy bowl and add the butter. Sift the flour with the dry ingredients. Beat the butter and sugar to a cream then start beating in the eggs, one at a time. Now add the fruit with a very little flour until it is all in. Beat in the rest of the flour and the brandy to make a soft mixture. Fill it into the tin keeping it well up at the sides and hollow at the centre. Place it in the oven at the second position from the bottom and turn down the heat at once to 300°F or Gas 2.

This cake should be cooked in 3 hours, but test with a skewer and give a little longer if necessary. The cake will keep for months in an airtight tin.

Almond Paste

½ lb ground almonds	2 teaspoonfuls lemon juice
½ lb icing sugar	½ teaspoonful vanilla essence
1 egg	

Sieve the icing sugar to make sure there are no lumps in it. Add the ground almonds to it and mix well; then form into a paste with the egg lightly beaten, the lemon juice and vanilla essence. Brush the cake to remove any loose crumbs and fill any cracks with a little of the paste, then brush over with warmed apricot jam.

Roll out half the paste to the size of the top of the cake, using icing sugar to flour the board. Put the paste on the top of the cake and level with the rolling pin well dusted with icing sugar. Roll out the other half of the paste in strips to fit the sides of the cake. Press neatly into position and make a join with jam. Take a jam jar and roll the sides with it to make them quite smooth. Trim the lower edge with a sharp knife. Allow 3 days to dry before putting on the royal icing.

Royal Icing

1 lb icing sugar
Whites of 2 eggs

½ teaspoonful lemon juice
1 tablespoonful glycerine

Sieve the icing sugar and stir it into the lightly beaten whites, lemon juice and glycerine. Beat steadily for at least 20 minutes or until you have a stiff consistency (the icing should stand in peaks). Use a palette knife dipped in hot water to ice the cake with long firm strokes, working the icing down the sides.

Leave it to dry before adding final decoration.

Castle Douglas Cake

½ lb plain white flour
4 oz butter
3 oz syrup
2 oz castor sugar
4 oz currants
4 oz sultanas

2 oz mixed peel
2 eggs
1 teaspoonful bicarbonate of soda
Finger-and-thumb of salt

Sift the flour with the salt and bicarbonate of soda. Beat the eggs well. Warm a baking bowl, and beat the syrup, sugar and butter in it to a cream. Add the fruit and the eggs and then work in the flour, beating well. Place in a lined cake tin and bake in a moderate oven for 1¼ hours.

Caraway Seed Cake

½ lb flour
4 oz castor sugar
4 oz butter
4 oz orange peel
4 eggs

1 teaspoonful baking powder
1 teaspoonful caraway seeds
1 teaspoonful sugar coated caraway seeds
Pinch of salt

Sift the flour with the baking powder and the salt. Beat the butter and the sugar to a cream. Beat the eggs well and cut the orange peel into very thin strips. Add the flour and the eggs to the beaten cream, and then add the peel and the caraway seeds. Beat well. Place in a well lined cake tin and sprinkle the coated seeds on top.

Bake in a moderate oven for 1¼ hours: when cooked the cake should be a light golden brown and firm to the touch on the top.

Miss McCaig's Christmas Cake

¾ lb plain white flour	4 oz mixed peel
½ lb butter	4 oz glacé cherries
½ lb castor sugar	1 tablespoonful treacle
½ lb sultanas	1 teaspoonful vanilla essence
½ lb muscatels	1 saltspoonful salt
½ lb currants	6 eggs

Clean the fruit and stone the muscatels. Shred the peel. Line the cake tin with greaseproof paper. Heat a roomy mixing bowl with very hot water, and beat the butter and sugar in it to a cream. Add the treacle, the vanilla essence and the salt; then start beating in the fruit and the eggs. When all the ingredients are in, start to beat in the flour.

This gives a creamy texture, neither runny nor stiff, which should be put into the lined tin, keeping it up at the sides and down in the centre. Preheat the oven to 550°F. Put the cake on the second position from the bottom and at once turn down the heat to 325°F. Cooking time: 2½ to 3 hours.

Fruit Fingers

8 oz currants	8 oz sultanas
2 oz sugar	1 tablespoonful lemon juice
4 oz peeled and cored weight	A little grated nutmeg
of apples	½ lb short crust paste

Pick over the currants and put them into a mixing bowl; add the sugar and the apples finely chopped. Mince the sultanas and add them. Add the nutmeg and the lemon juice and mix well.

Divide the paste into two and roll the pieces out the same size. Lay one on a baking sheet, spread the mixture over it, not quite to the edges. Damp the edges with cold water and lay the other piece on top. Press the edges together firmly.

Prick evenly over with a fork then brush lightly with beaten egg. Dust heavily with castor sugar. Bake in a moderate oven for 20 to 30 minutes. When brown and the fruit is oozing juice a little it is ready.

When quite cold, cut in fingers.

Date Fingers

This is made exactly as fruit fingers with the following filling:

2 oz butter
4 oz currants
4 oz chopped dates

2 oz sugar
½ teaspoonful ground ginger
½ teaspoonful ground cinnamon

Melt the butter in a saucepan, add the other ingredients and stir until hot. Cool a little before spreading on the paste.

A Cake for Oidhche Challain: (Hogmany)

½ lb butter
½ lb icing sugar
12 oz plain white flour
1 lb currants
½ lb mixed peel, lemon, citron, orange

1 teaspoonful mixed spice
1 saltspoonful Jamaica pepper
1 saltspoonful salt
4 tablespoonfuls brandy
6 eggs

Sift the flour well with the salt and the spices. Wash and pick over the currants making sure they are thoroughly dried. Shred the peel finely and sift the icing sugar to make sure there are no lumps in it. Beat the butter and the sugar until it is white and foamy, then beat in the eggs and the fruit. Keep beating steadily, add a very little flour with the fruit, then start adding the rest of the flour and the brandy.

Double line a cake tin and fill the mixture into it, keeping it up at the sides and down in the middle. Let it sit for 20 minutes.

This was a cake that was cooked according to the weight of the mixture, which is about 4 lb. It was baked in a slow oven for 4 hours. However, I prefer to preheat an electric oven to 550°F, put the cake on the second position from the bottom and at once turn the heat down to 325°F; the cake should cook evenly and perfectly in 2¾ hours.

To finish the cake, cover with almond icing and then royal icing as in the recipe for Christmas cake.

Dundee Cake

10 oz plain white flour	4 oz raisins
6 oz castor sugar	2 oz mixed peel
6 oz butter	2 oz ground almonds
4 eggs	1 oz whole almonds
4 oz currants	1 teaspoonful baking powder
4 oz sultanas	1 saltspoonful salt

Drop the whole almonds into a pan of boiling water and leave them for a minute; then peel and split them. Beat the butter and sugar to a cream and then beat in the eggs, one at a time, along with the ground almonds. Sift the flour with the salt and baking powder and gradually add it to the creamed mixture along with the fruit and peel, chopped. Put the mixture into a lined cake tin, smooth it over and arrange the split almonds on top.

Preheat the oven to 500°F, put the cake in (second position from the bottom) and at once lower the heat to 325°F. Bake for 1½ hours. Then take it out gently and listen to it: if it is 'purring' it is still cooking so put it back and listen occasionally until the 'purring' stops.

Doughnuts

½ lb plain white flour	2 oz butter
A pinch of salt	1 egg
1 teaspoonful baking powder, neither heaped nor level	1 tablespoonful milk
1 tablespoonful castor sugar	3 drops vanilla essence

Beat the egg well, add the milk and the essence to it. Sift the flour, salt and baking powder and add the sugar. Rub in the butter until the mixture is like fine breadcrumbs and mix to a firm dough with the egg and milk mixture. (It may take a little more milk but this is unlikely). Roll out the dough, fairly thick, on a floured board. Cut into rounds with a cutter and with a smaller one cut out the centre.

Have a deep frying pan almost half full of cooking fat just at the faint blue smoke stage and with a frying basket for preference. Place as many doughnuts as the basket will hold without crowding and lower it into the fat. Turn them from time to time until they are a golden brown all round.

Turn the doughnuts out on a piece of greaseproof paper on an ashet then toss them quickly in castor sugar.

Doughnuts with Jam

Roll out the dough much thinner and, using a large ring, cut in rounds. Damp the edges all round with milk, put a teaspoonful of jam on one half and fold over the other (as for jam turnovers). Pinch the edges to seal them and fry them in fat not quite so hot as for doughnuts with a hole in them.

Drain on paper and toss in castor sugar to which some ground cinnamon has been added.

Doughnuts with Yeast

½ lb plain white flour	2 eggs
½ oz yeast	1 oz butter
1 oz sugar	1 gill milk

Warm a bowl with warm water, break the eggs into it, and beat them well. Warm the milk to blood heat and add it to the eggs, then cream the yeast with the sugar and add it. Rub the butter into the flour, add the liquid and make a light easily handled dough. Set to rise.

When well risen take small portions of the dough (this quantity should make a dozen doughnuts) put a spot of a very firm jam in the centre and fold over and make into a round ball. Give them 15 minutes to prove in a warm corner.

Meanwhile get the deep fat ready (it should be at a faint blue smoke temperature). Fry the doughnuts turning them all the time until they are an overall golden brown for just under 5 minutes. Drain on greaseproof paper and toss in castor sugar.

Gingerbreads

There are dozens of recipes for gingerbread: some of the old Scots recipes have beer in them, some have honey, some have cream, some buttermilk and many have oatmeal. Many of course were steamed, others were baked in an oven pot with a glowing peat on the lid.

12

Carlisle Gingerbread

4 oz lard
4 oz butter
8 oz soft brown sugar
4 tablespoonfuls treacle
1 lb plain white flour
2 teaspoonfuls ground ginger
2 teaspoonfuls ground cinnamon
2 teaspoonfuls mixed spice

1 saltspoonful ground cloves
1 saltspoonful ground nutmeg
1 saltspoonful Jamaica pepper
1 saltspoonful salt
2 eggs
1 teaspoonful bicarbonate of
    soda melted in a half cupful
    warm water

Melt the lard, sugar, butter and treacle in a saucepan (there is no
need to bring it to the boil). Sift the flour two or three times with
the spices. Beat the eggs in a roomy bowl, pour the melted mixture
over them, beating well, and then work in the flour. Add the water
with the bicarbonate of soda last. The mixture should be a pouring
consistency and can be poured into a lined cake tin.

Bake at 350°F or Gas Mark 4 for 1 hour.

Miss McCulloch's Gingerbread

1½ lb plain white flour
4 oz soft brown sugar
1 lb treacle
½ lb butter
3 eggs
¼ pint of milk

1 oz ground ginger
½ oz mixed spice
Pinch of salt
1 teaspoonful bicarbonate of
    soda

Sift the flour with the spices, the sugar and the salt. Liquify the
milk, treacle and butter in a pan but do not heat them past melting
point. Beat the eggs well and add them to the mixture and then
start working it into the flour. Beat well, then melt the bicarbonate
of soda in a spoonful of milk and add this last.

Pour into a well lined cake tin and bake in a moderate oven for
1½ to 2 hours. The cake should be firm to the touch when ready;
this is a moist gingerbread.

Miss Cryle's Gingerbread

2 eggs
6 oz plain white flour
2 oz fine oatmeal
4 oz butter
3 oz soft brown sugar
2 tablespoonfuls treacle

½ teaspoonful each of bicarbonate of soda, mixed spice and ground cinnamon
1 heaped teaspoonful ground ginger
Saltspoonful of salt

Beat the butter and the sugar to a cream and then beat in the treacle. Dip the spoon in boiling water and the treacle will slip off cleanly. Beat the eggs. Sift the flour with the spices and salt (but not the bicarbonate of soda). Mix the flour and the oatmeal and work into the creamed mixture, with the eggs. Dissolve the soda in a tablespoonful of milk and add it last.

Spoon the mixture into a lined tin and bake in a moderate oven for 1 hour.

Drumlanrig Gingerbread

8 oz of fine oatmeal
8 oz plain white flour
4 oz soft brown sugar
6 oz lard
4 oz syrup
2 eggs

1 teaspoonful of bicarbonate of soda
1 heaped teaspoonful ground ginger
Saltspoonful of salt

Sift the flour with the bicarbonate of soda, the salt, the sugar and the ginger and add the oatmeal to it. Melt the syrup and the lard enough to make them runny. Beat the eggs and add them, and then make a soft dough with them, adding the mixture slowly to the flour mixture.

Pour into a lined tin and bake in a moderate oven. Time: just over 1 hour.

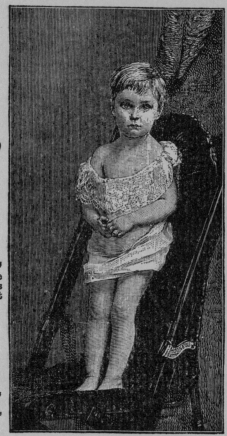

A Fruit Gingerbread

1 lb plain white flour
½ lb butter
½ lb demerara sugar
4 oz treacle
4 oz syrup
4 eggs
4 oz currants
4 oz sultanas
4 oz mixed peel

2 oz preserved ginger
1 teaspoonful bicarbonate of soda
1 teaspoonful ground cinnamon
2 teaspoonfuls ground ginger
½ teaspoonful ground nutmeg
½ teaspoonful ground cloves
Saltspoonful Jamaica pepper
Saltspoonful salt

Sift the flour with all the spices and the bicarbonate of soda. Sieve it two or three times to make sure the spices are well mixed. Melt the syrup, treacle, sugar and butter, stirring all the time until it comes through the boil. Have the eggs well beaten in a roomy bowl and pour the boiling mixture over them, beating vigorously all the time.

Now put all the flour into the mixture and beat until quite smooth. Then start to add in the prepared fruit, the peel shredded and the ginger thinly sliced.

Pour into a lined cake tin and bake in a moderate oven for 2 hours.

Spiced Cake

1 lb plain white flour
6 oz butter
4 oz sugar
¼ lb currants
½ lb sultanas
2 oz mixed peel
¾ teaspoonful tartaric acid
1 teaspoonful bicarbonate of soda

Half a nutmeg grated
1 heaped teaspoonful mixed spice
A pinch of salt
4 eggs
2 tablespoonfuls treacle
2 tablespoonfuls milk

Sift the flour into a roomy bowl and add the butter and sugar. Rub the butter into the flour until the mixture is as fine as you can make it. Add the fruit. Beat the eggs thoroughly. Just warm the milk enough to melt the treacle and mix in all the spices, acid, soda and salt. Pour this into the eggs and mix into the flour, beating well.

Bake in a lined cake tin in a fairly hot oven to begin with, then lower the heat after 30 minutes. Time in all: 2 hours.

Spiced Cake (without eggs)

4 oz soft brown sugar
4 oz butter
4 oz mixed fruit
4 oz syrup
½ teaspoonful ground cinnamon
½ teaspoonful mixed spice

½ teaspoonful ground ginger
½ teaspoonful ground cloves
½ teaspoonful bicarbonate of soda
½ teacupful milk
¼ lb flour

Beat the butter and sugar to a cream, slightly heat the syrup and beat it in, then add the milk. Add the fruit and last the flour well sifted with the spices and the soda.

Bake in a lined cake tin, in a moderate oven for 1¼ hours..

Icing a Cake

Royal Icing

1 lb icing sugar
4 whites of eggs

1 dessertspoonful lemon juice
A little washing blue

All icing sugar must be sifted through a fine sieve. The lemon juice must be strained and measured after straining. Beat the whites of the eggs a little in a clean deepish roomy bowl. Slowly add the icing sugar, beating with deep movements and cleaving in air with every stroke. When half the sugar is in add the lemon juice and continue beating. Then add a few drops of washing blue. This gives the icing that purity of whiteness. Go on beating until the icing is stiff enough to stand up in a peak on the spoon.

If you are not quite ready to ice the cake, cover the icing with a damp cloth and leave it in a cool place until you can use it. Do not allow the icing to come into contact with the cloth (a spurtle across the mouth of the bowl would prevent this).

Oatmeal Loaf

½ lb oatmeal
10 oz plain white flour
½ teaspoonful salt

1 teaspoonful bicarbonate of
  soda
2 teaspoonfuls cream of tartar
¾ pint milk

Soak the oatmeal in the milk overnight. Sift the flour with the raising agents and stir it into the oatmeal mixture. This should be a very soft mixture.

Pour it into a heavily buttered loaf tin and bake in a moderate oven for 1½ hours.

Oven Oat Bannocks

½ lb fine oatmeal
¼ lb plain white flour
4 oz butter

1 heaped teaspoonful baking
  powder
½ teaspoonful salt
1 teaspoonful castor sugar

Put all the dry ingredients into a baking bowl and rub in the butter until the mixture is like fine breadcrumbs. Add enough cold water to mix to a firm dough. Knead lightly and then roll out on a floured board in a fairly thick round.

Cut in eight pieces and bake on a greased baking sheet in a moderate oven for 20 minutes.

Ginger Sponge (1)

½ lb plain white flour
½ teaspoonful baking powder
¼ teaspoonful bicarbonate of
  soda
A good pinch of salt

4 oz soft brown sugar
2 oz lard
1 tablespoonful syrup
½ teacupful milk
1 egg

Sift the flour with the baking powder, the soda and the salt. Rub in the sugar through the flour, making sure there are no lumps. Put the milk into a pan, add the lard and syrup and warm just enough to melt the lard and syrup. Beat the egg well, pour the liquid mixture over it and then stir this into the flour, using a beating movement to make a soft mixture.

Pour it into a well greased tin and bake for 30 minutes in a moderate oven.

Ginger Sponge (2)

1 lb plain white flour
½ lb soft brown sugar
½ lb butter
1 cupful milk
1 cupful syrup
Saltspoonful salt

1 heaped teaspoonful bicarbonate of soda
2 heaped teaspoonfuls ground
ginger
4 eggs

Dissolve the bicarbonate of soda in a little of the milk. Put the rest of the milk into a saucepan and add the syrup. Make it a nice runny mixture but do not make it hot. Sift the flour with the salt and the ground ginger. Beat the butter and sugar to a good creamy mixture, working in the syrup and milk. Beat the eggs well and start working in the flour and the eggs. Finally add the bicarbonate to the milk.

Pour into a lined cake tin and bake in a moderate oven for 1 hour (it may take a little longer). A light touch with the finger will tell you if it is cooked. (This cake is excellent with a ginger butter icing.)

Ginger Butter Icing

½ lb icing sugar   3 oz butter
1 tablespoonful ginger essence

Beat the butter and the sugar together, gradually adding the essence. Spread evenly on top and decorate with slivers of crystallised ginger. Make sure there are no lumps in the icing sugar.

Baking a Sponge Cake

5 oz plain white flour
4 oz butter
3 oz castor sugar
2 eggs

1 tablespoonful milk
1 level teaspoonful baking powder

Preheat the oven to 400°F. Line the cake tin with greaseproof paper. Warm a baking bowl with very hot water and put the butter and sugar into it. Sift the flour with the baking powder and the salt. Beat the eggs well. Beat the butter and the sugar until it is white and foamy. Beat in the eggs and then fold in the flour, adding the milk slowly. This should be a moist dropping mixture. Fill it into the tin.

Cook in the oven, second shelf from the bottom, lower the heat to 350°F (Gas Mark 4) for 1 hour.

Mocha Cake

4 oz flour
4 oz castor sugar
2 oz butter
2 eggs

1 teaspoonful baking powder (level)
3 dessertspoonfuls milk
Apricot jam
A pinch of salt

Line a cake tin with greaseproof paper and set the oven at 'moderate'. Beat the butter and sugar to a cream and separate the eggs. Beat the yolks well and add the milk to them. Beat the whites until stiff. Work the flour into the creamed butter along with the yolks and milk, then add the baking powder and salt. Last fold in the whites gently, pile into the tin and bake until it is a pale golden brown and firm to the touch: it will not take more than 30 minutes, perhaps even less.

When quite cold, cut through the middle and spread freely with apricot jam. Coat with coffee icing and pipe a decoration.

Coffee Icing

2 oz fresh butter
4 oz icing sugar

1 tablespoonful strong black coffee
3 drops vanilla essence

Soften the butter in a warm mixing bowl and beat it a little. Sift the icing sugar on to it and beat it until creamy; then slowly add the coffee, beating all the time.

When thoroughly mixed, spread over the cake, using about half of it. Use the rest to pipe a decoration. If by chance you curdle the icing, work in a little more sifted icing sugar.

Orange Sandwich

4 oz butter
4 oz sugar
4 oz flour

$\frac{1}{2}$ teaspoonful baking powder
Pinch of salt
2 eggs

Grease and dust with flour two sandwich tins. Sift the flour, powder and salt: since it is a small quantity of flour it is wise to sift this twice to get the baking powder right through it. Beat the butter and sugar to a cream, drop in the eggs and beat well. Then mix in the sifted flour. Divide evenly between the two tins.

Bake in a moderate oven for 20 minutes. A light touch will tell you if the sponges are cooked. To heighten the orange flavour of the finished cake you can mix into the dough the grated rind of one orange.

Orange Butter Filling

8 oz icing sugar
2 oz butter

Orange juice

Soften the butter a little and just warm the juice of the orange. Sift the icing sugar and beat it in, adding a little more juice if necessary Colour lightly with an orange colour.

Orange Icing

8 oz icing sugar
Orange juice

Colouring

Sift the icing sugar and strain the orange juice. Add orange juice to the icing until you have a spreading consistency which is not too runny. Cover the sandwich and leave to set.

This sandwich should be kept now for at least one day as it mellows with keeping.

Orange Sandwich Cake

2 oz plain white flour	Small teaspoonful baking
1 oz cornflour	powder
3 oz castor sugar	Rind of one orange
3 eggs	

Sift the flour with the baking powder and cornflour. Put the eggs and sugar into a bowl and set this bowl into a larger one with hot water in it. Beat the egg and sugar until it is white and frothy and take the smaller bowl out of the water. Fold in the flour and the rind of orange finely grated.

Butter two sandwich tins, shake a little flour over them and then shake it out again. Evenly divide the sponge mixture between them, and bake in a moderately hot oven for 15 minutes. They should be a pale golden brown and firm to the touch. Turn out on a wire tray.

To serve, fill with beaten cream very lightly flavoured with sugar and coat with icing made with:

Juice of the orange	Icing sugar
Teaspoonful butter	

Warm the juice sufficiently to melt the butter and then work in the sifted icing sugar until it is of a spreading consistency.

Sponge Sandwich

3 eggs	$\frac{1}{2}$ teaspoonful cream of tartar
4 oz castor sugar	$\frac{1}{4}$ teaspoonful bicarbonate of
3 oz plain white flour	soda

Break the eggs into a deepish bowl and add the sugar. Put some very hot water into a bigger bowl and set the bowl with the eggs in it: but do not have so much water that the smaller bowl floats in it. Beat the eggs and the sugar until it is an almost firm, frothy mixture. Have the flour sifted with the raising agents and fold this into the beaten eggs (do not beat any more).

Butter two sandwich tins and then dust lightly with flour and divide the mixture evenly between the tins.

Bake in an oven heated to 375°F or gas Mark 5 for 15 minutes (a light touch with the finger will tell you if the sponges are quite cooked). Let the sponges sit for a few minutes before turning them out.

Ginger Nuts

1 lb plain white flour	A pinch of salt
2 teaspoonfuls ground ginger	6 oz butter
1 heaped teaspoonful bicar- bonate of soda	6 oz castor sugar
	4 tablespoonfuls syrup

Sift the flour with the soda, salt and ginger. Put the butter into a mixing bowl and add the sugar; beat lightly then beat in the syrup. Work in the flour until it is a firm dough. Then roll it out on a well floured board, fairly thick.

Cut in rounds and bake in a fairly brisk oven until a golden brown. Leave on the baking sheet for a little after taking from the oven before lifting.

Parkins (1)

6 oz plain white flour	$\frac{1}{2}$ teaspoonful ground cinnamon
6 oz fine oatmeal	A smallish teaspoonful bicar- bonate of soda
$2\frac{1}{2}$ oz soft brown sugar	Pinch of salt
2 oz butter	1 egg
1 teaspoonful ground ginger	3 oz syrup
$\frac{1}{2}$ teaspoonful mixed spice	

Sift the flour with the spices and the bicarbonate of soda. Add the sugar, rub in the butter and then add the oatmeal. Trickle the syrup through the mixture and then bind it to a soft dough with the beaten egg.

Flour the hands and make the mixture into little balls. Flatten them a little before putting them well apart on a greased baking sheet.

Bake until brown and crinkly in a moderate oven.

Parkins (2)

4 oz fine oatmeal	3 oz good dripping or butter
4 oz plain white flour	½ teaspoonful mixed spice
2 oz brown sugar	1 teaspoonful baking powder
2 tablespoonfuls treacle	Almonds

Mix well the oatmeal, flour, spice and baking powder in a baking bowl. Warm and melt the dripping, treacle and sugar in a pan. Stir this mixture into the flour and mix well. Grease a baking sheet. Take about a dessertspoonful of the mixture and form into a ball. Repeat until the mixture is used up. Keep them well apart on the baking sheet as they will spread.

Put split and blanched almonds on top of each parkin and bake in a moderate oven for about 20 minutes until they are brown.

Parkins (3)

½ lb fine oatmeal	3 oz good dripping or butter
¼ lb flour	½ teaspoonful ground ginger
3 oz margarine	½ teaspoonful mixed spice
2 tablespoonfuls syrup	½ teaspoonful ground cinnamon
2 tablespoonfuls treacle	3 oz castor sugar

Mix all the ingredients thoroughly and if you think the mixture is going to be too stiff, add a spoonful of milk. Shape into balls and place them well apart on a greased baking sheet.

Bake in a moderate oven until brown (about 20 minutes).

Oatcakes (with boiling water)

1 lb fine oatmeal
1 tablespoonful liquid fat
1 teaspoonful bicarbonate of
    soda

A saltspoonful salt
Boiling water

Good dripping or bacon fat is ideal for oatcakes, and must be melted before using. Put the oatmeal into a bowl, add the salt and bicarbonate of soda, then pour in the fat and mix a little. Now quickly pour in enough boiling water to make a soft dough and roll into a lump.

Scatter oatmeal over a baking board, and knead the dough on it, working it to a smooth ball. Spread the dough out with the knuckles, sprinkling oatmeal over and under as required. Then roll it out to about ⅛ inch in thickness. Use the palm of the hand to rub off most of the oatmeal then brush it over.

Cut the cakes into triangles and bake on a fairly hot girdle, turning the cakes when they are brown. Finish off in front of the fire or in a hot oven.

Oatcakes (with buttermilk)

For one round of oatcakes put two handfuls of oatmeal into a bowl, add a pinch of salt and as much bicarbonate of soda as you can lift between your finger and thumb. Make into a soft dough with ½ cup of buttermilk.

Roll out and bake on a hot girdle and then finish in front of the fire or in a hot oven.

Maggie Ross's Biscuits

6 oz fine oatmeal
5 oz plain white flour
4 oz icing sugar
3 oz butter
2 tablespoonfuls milk

1 egg
1 teaspoonful, neither heaped
nor level, of baking powder
A saltspoonful of salt

Sieve the sugar, the flour, the salt and the baking powder into a large bowl. Rub in the butter until the mixture is very fine before adding the oatmeal. Beat the egg well and add the milk to it. Pour this into the mixture and make it into a firm dough. Knead it well then roll it out fairly thinly on a well floured baking board. Cut into rounds, any size you like (a 3 inch cutter is a good size). Most biscuits have to be well dabbed with a fork or with a cutter specially made for the job, but not this one.

Grease a baking sheet well as the biscuits tend to stick a little. Bake until they are a pale golden brown at 375°F or mark 5.

Oatmeal Biscuits

4 oz plain white flour
4 oz fine oatmeal
3 oz butter

1 oz castor sugar
1 teaspoonful baking powder
A saltspoonful of salt

Put all the dry ingredients into the baking bowl and rub in the butter. Add enough milk to make a stiff dough and knead until it is smooth. Roll it out thinly, cut in rounds and bake in a moderate oven until the biscuits are a pale golden brown.

Digestive Biscuits

½ lb barley flour
½ lb fine oatmeal
2 oz lard
2 oz butter
½ teacupful bicarbonate of soda

Saltspoonful of salt
1 dessertspoonful castor sugar
1 egg
Milk

Mix the dry ingredients, rub in the butter and lard and make into a stiff dough with the beaten egg and a spoonful of milk. Knead until smooth and then roll out thinly. Cut in rounds and dab all over with a fork.

Bake in a moderate oven until the cakes are a pale golden brown.

To Mould Shortbread

If the mould is new it must be 'tempered'. To do this wash it well, dry it thoroughly, and then brush it with salad oil. Wipe off surplus oil with a clean dry cloth and the mould is ready for use. (It need not be washed or oiled again if it is stored in a clean cupboard where it cannot become dusty.)

Before use, dust it liberally with castor or sifted sugar, tilting the mould to get the sugar into every cranny, then give it a sharp 'dunt' on the table to remove surplus sugar.

Shortbread dough for moulding must be really firm yet pliable. Roll out the dough in the round slightly smaller than the size of the mould so that the dough fits neatly into the depression, put it in the mould and roll firmly with the rolling pin. Have a dry, un-greased baking tin at the ready. With the fingertips free the short-bread round the edges, upturn the mould on the baking tin, give a sharp 'dunt' with the rolling pin and the shortbread with its attractive pattern should be on the baking sheet.

Almond Shortbread

14 oz plain white flour   8 oz butter
2 oz rice flour   4 oz castor sugar
2 oz ground almonds

Sift the flours and almonds together. Put the butter on a marble baking slab or a floured baking board. Knead the sugar into it and then start to work in the flours. Knead steadily until all the flours are in and you have a soft, pliable dough which should then be divided into two. Press out with the hands, then press firmly and evenly into a well-floured shortbread mould. Leave the shortbread on a cool baking sheet for an hour to ripen, then prick all over with a fork.

Bake in a moderate oven until the cakes are a pale golden brown.

Edinburgh Shortbread

12 oz plain white flour   8 oz butter
4 oz rice flour   4 oz castor sugar

Sift the two flours twice. Beat the butter and the sugar to a cream in a warm mixing bowl. Start working in the flours: if you think it is becoming too firm and crumbly do not add all the flour. However, you should not have more than 2 oz over. Knead the paste until it is quite smooth, then roll it out on a floured board. Cut into two squares, dab all over with a fork and pinch the edges with the forefinger and thumb. Leave for an hour to set.

Bake in a moderate oven until the cakes are a pale golden brown.

Petticoat Tails

This recipe is from a West Highland baker who used it for thirty years in Victorian days.

1 lb fine white flour   4 oz pounded sugar
6 oz best butter   2 oz unsalted lard

Put all the ingredients into a bowl and rub between the palms of the hands until the mixture is like fine breadcrumbs. Gather in a heap and bind in a lump by pressing with the left hand down on the right until the texture is right. No moisture should be added. Divide into four. Roll out each piece on a floured board, keeping in the round. Pierce with a sharp fork all over and crimp the edges with the finger and thumb. Now take a small cutter and cut out the centre and put it on a baking sheet. Cut the piece left into twelve 'tails' and arrange on the baking sheet round the circle. This is the true petticoat tail arrangement. Repeat with the other pieces.

Bake in a pre-heated oven of moderate temperature until golden brown.

Author's note: I find this easier to handle if less flour is used to begin with and more added when forming the dough, if needed. Dough must be firm and cut sharp and clean.

Yule Bannock

1 lb plain white flour 8 oz butter
4 oz icing sugar   A pinch of salt
2 oz lemon and orange peel 4 drops vanilla essence
2 oz almonds

For this bannock you must have whole peel cut in very thin strips. Blanch the almonds and cut them in thin chips. Sieve the flour into a roomy baking bowl, add the peel, the nuts, the salt, the sugar and the essence. Melt the butter without overheating it, and pour it into the mixture in the bowl. Work it quickly into a dough and add a little more flour if you think it is on the soft side. Turn the dough out on a floured board and divide it evenly in two.

Knead each piece in the round until it is about ½ inch thick. Pinch round the edges with the finger and thumb and then prick all over with a fork, avoiding the fruit and nuts if possible.

Let them rest for some hours in a cool larder then bake rather slowly in a moderate oven until the cakes are a pale golden brown.

Yule Shortbread

½ lb plain white flour 4 oz icing sugar
2 oz rice flour   1 teaspoonful vanilla essence
6 oz butter

Mix the two flours together. Sift the icing sugar into a baking bowl and add the butter and the vanilla essence. Beat to a cream and then work in the flours. Knead until smooth and then put out on to a floured board. Knead it out a little, working the shape into a square, then roll it out until it is about ½ inch thick. Flute the edges with the finger and thumb and prick all over the cake with a fork.

Pre-heat the oven to 350°F and bake the shortbread until it is a pale golden brown. When it is quite cold, decorate with icing.

Icing

6 oz icing sugar   The juice of ¼ a lemon
The white of 1 egg

Sift the sugar. Beat the white of egg a little, and add the sugar and lemon juice to it. Beat until quite stiff. Work a scroll round the edge of the cake and pipe in the centre.

'A Guid New Year.'

Coating Cake with Icing

The cake must be quite even across the top: if it is not, it must be trimmed until it is. Brush it with a soft brush to remove any loose crumbs. Some cakes are covered with marzipan before being iced, but here I will deal with a cake without marzipan. A revolving cake stand is ideal for icing but not essential.

Put the cake on a cake tin, a size smaller than the cake itself. Lift a good spoonful of icing, put it on top of the cake and with a palette knife or a broad table knife spread the icing quite roughly over the cake. Then place the point of the knife, free from icing sugar, in the centre of the cake, holding it steadily, horizontally, with the right hand. Take the point in the left hand and swing the knife evenly round in one direction. If the icing is not even, put on some more and work again until it is smooth. Work icing round the sides and with the knife at a slant smooth them off. Leave the cake in a cool place to allow it to set.

If cake is to be decorated with piping, the same icing can be used.

Glacé Icing

Glacé icing is a soft icing and is easily made. As with other icings, the sugar must be sifted through a very fine sieve. Proportions: $\frac{1}{2}$ lb icing sugar to 3 tablespoonfuls warm water.

Put the sugar into a bowl and slowly add the water (it may not take quite all of it). Mix until it will coat the back of the spoon.

Colour and flavouring can be added as desired, but if much liquid is involved, allow for it in the measure of water.

Coffee Icing

Use clear black coffee, tepid, to mix with the sugar.

Chocolate Icing

Dissolve $1\frac{1}{2}$ oz of cooking chocolate in the water. Some cooks used to add a piece of butter, about the size of a nutmeg to 3 tablespoonfuls of water for glacé icing.

Note: If the water is too hot, and the icing overheated, it will remain dull looking.

Mrs Nelson's Cream Scones

1½ breakfast cupfuls flour
1 teaspoonful baking powder
Pinch of salt

Piece of butter the size of a large egg
1 teaspoonful sugar
1 cup of thin cream

Sift the flour, salt and baking powder into a baking bowl. Add the sugar, rub the butter into the flour and make it into a soft dough with the cream. Work quickly and divide the dough into two.

Roll out one and bake it on a hot girdle, first on one side and then on the other. While it is baking, roll out the second round. Put the scones into a clean towel as they come from the girdle.

Miss Murray's Scones

1 lb plain white flour
4 oz butter
2 heaped teaspoonfuls baking powder

Pinch of salt
1 egg
Just under ½ pint milk

Sift the flour with the salt and the baking powder, and rub in the butter until the mixture is very fine. Beat the egg until light and frothy, add the milk to it and pour into the flour. Work it quickly into a dough and knead lightly.

Roll out on a floured board to 1 inch in thickness and cut into rounds. Flour freely and bake in a hot oven for 15 minutes.

If preferred, instead of flouring the scones, keep them reasonably free of flour, and brush with beaten egg before putting into the oven.

Girdle Wholemeal Scones

½ lb wholemeal flour
½ teaspoonful bicarbonate of
  soda
1 teaspoonful cream of tartar
A pinch of salt

2 teaspoonfuls castor sugar *or*
  a tablespoonful syrup
1 oz margarine or butter
Milk to mix

Put the flour into a baking bowl. Sift in the raising agents to avoid lumps. Add the sugar now; but if you use syrup add it with the milk. Rub in the margarine and add just enough milk to make a soft dough and turn it out on a floured board. Knead it a little, keeping it in the round, and then roll it out ½ inch thick.

Cut in eight and bake on a hot girdle, first on one side and then on the other.

Treacle Scones

½ lb plain white flour
½ teaspoonful bicarbonate of
  soda
1 teaspoonful cream of tartar
Pinch of salt
½ teaspoonful ground ginger

¼ teaspoonful ground cinnamon
¼ teaspoonful mixed spice
1 tablespoonful treacle
1 tablespoonful soft brown sugar
2 oz butter
Milk

Sift the flour with all the dry ingredients. Rub in the butter and trickle the treacle through the mixture until it is in fine threads: then add just enough milk to make a soft dough.

Roll it out on a floured board, cut it in eight triangles and bake in a hot oven for just under 15 minutes.

Girdle Pancakes: Fat

8 oz plain white flour
1 teaspoonful cream of tartar
½ teaspoonful bicarbonate of
  soda
A pinch of salt

A dessertspoonful oiled butter
2 eggs
2 oz castor sugar
½ pint milk less 1 tablespoonful

Sift the flour with the raising agents and the salt. Beat the eggs, the sugar and the butter to a foamy cream, begin to beat in the flour and slowly add milk at the same time. The batter should be the consistency of thick cream, but light and buoyant.

Bake as for thin pancakes on a hot greased girdle.

Girdle Pancakes: Thin

8 oz flour	1 oz castor sugar
1 egg	1 small teaspoonful bicarbonate
Pinch of salt	of soda
½ pint milk	Twice that of cream of tartar

Sieve the flour and the salt into a basin and make a batter by gradually working in half of the milk. Add the egg yolk and beat well for 5 minutes. Sift the cream of tartar and bicarbonate of soda into a bowl to make sure there are no lumps, then add the rest of the milk to them. Beat this into the batter. Beat the white of the egg until stiff and fold it into the batter last.

Grease a hot girdle with a piece of suet and drop spoonfuls of the batter on the girdle. When the surface falls into little holes, turn the pancake and brown on the other side. Grease the girdle well after each batch.

Wholemeal Scones (with yeast)

½ lb wholemeal flour	½ pint milk
½ lb plain white flour	1 dessertspoonful sugar
1½ teaspoonfuls salt	3 oz butter
1 oz yeast	

Mix the flours well, add the salt and rub in the butter. Cream the yeast with the sugar and add the milk heated to blood temperature. Pour this into the flour and mix well then knead it lightly a little. Cover the basin with a warm towel and set it in a warm corner of the kitchen for an hour (up on a shelf is always a good place as heat rises). The dough should rise to twice its size.

Flour a board, turn out the dough and knead it lightly again. Roll it out, cut it in the desired shape and put the scones on a warm baking sheet to prove.

Bake in a hot oven until brown. Time: 15 minutes.

Potato Pastry

Potato pastry is excellent for pasties, little meat pies, plate pies with minced meat and even macaroni with bacon or cheese.

½ lb plain white flour	1 teaspoonful baking powder
6 oz mashed potatoes	A pinch of salt and cold water
4 oz butter	to mix

Peel and boil the potatoes without salt. Shake them well to dry them and make them floury: then mash them until they are quite smooth. Cream the butter in a warmed bowl. Work in the potato and then the flour with the salt and the baking powder sifted through it. Add just enough cold water to mix; it will not take very much so do not drown the miller.

Roll out as for ordinary pastry.

Potato Scones

½ lb cooked potato	1 tablespoonful milk
2 oz flour	Pinch of salt

Boil the potatoes until tender, then shake and dry well before mashing them. Have them very smooth and add a very little salt. Now work in the flour (it may take a little more than the given quantity) and add just enough milk to make a stiff dough.

Roll out very thin on a well floured board. Cut into rounds and prick with a fork. Bake on a hot girdle, first on one side and then on the other. This takes about 5 minutes and they do not take on an even brown.

Serve hot with butter.

Potato and Oatmeal Cakes

Boil and drain thoroughly some potatoes. Shake them well to get them dry and mealy, and mash until there are no lumps left. Add enough fine oatmeal to make a rolling out consistency and add a little salt if necessary. Roll out on a well floured board, prick with a fork and cut in four. Cook, first on one side and then on the other on a hot girdle.

Yeast

Yeast is fascinating to work with. You can buy dried yeast, or you may be able to buy compressed yeast from a yeast merchant or your baker. Yeast works on the 'no food, no work' principle, since it is a form of plant life and sugar is the food required. Heat is also necessary to stimulate activity.

Action is started by creaming the yeast: the required amount of yeast is put into a warm bowl, a teaspoonful of sugar is added and the two are worked together. In a short time the yeast liquifies. When it is added to a dough it attacks the sugar in the dough and brings about a chemical action which breaks up the sugar and forms carbon dioxide and alcohol; the result is fermentation, which cannot be brought about without heat.

Bowls, tins, baking sheets should have the chill taken off them before being used for yeast dough. Flour absorbs the temperature of the room in which it is stored and it is wise to have flour for any baking in a warm atmosphere overnight. There are three terms you may find in a recipe using yeast: creaming, setting to sponge, and proving.

1 Set to Sponge

The yeast, creamed and mixed with warm milk, is poured into a well in the centre of the flour and left like that in a warm place for 20 minutes without mixing at all. After that time the dough is mixed, other ingredients may be added, and the whole kneaded before the dough is set to rise.

2 Proving

Proving is the rising after the dough has been shaped into buns, loaves, as the case may be. They are put on a warm baking sheet and left in a warm place for 15 minutes. This gives them a chance to rise again after kneading and further fermentation takes place.

Puddings and
Sweets

Brandy and Chestnut Whip: Colonel Cameron's

2 lb chestnuts

2 tablespoonfuls brandy

Fully ½ pint double cream

Vanilla flavoured sugar

Cut the shell of the nuts with a sharp knife and put them in the oven to crack. Shell them. Parboil them to remove the skin then cook gently in plenty of boiling water with just a suspicion of salt. When soft, drain them. Set a sieve over a wide basin and rub the chestnuts through it, avoiding making them into a paste. In another bowl whip the cream gradually adding the brandy and sugar to taste. Three to four ounces may be required but avoid over-sweetening. Now take a spoon and fold in spoonfuls of the chestnut, but not all of it. Leave enough to make a small decoration on each cup to be served. Pile into the cups in which it will be served. Now make a paste with a little more sugar and brandy of the remaining chestnut. Make any form of it you like to top the whip.

Serve very cold with fine wafers.

Note: The mixture can be made to resemble chestnuts and angelica cut to make leaves.

Baked Apples: Colonel Cameron's

Choose large well rounded apples of the same size. Drop them into a bowl of boiling water and this will let you take off a paper-thin peeling. Core them. Take a fork and rasp the sides of the apples and roll them forcefully in a bowl of rough brown sugar.

Put them on a fireproof dish well greased and fill them with the following 'plug'.

Break down one or two sponge biscuits, add some brown sugar, a few currants and, with a fork, work in a piece of butter and then moisten with rum. Roll into 'cores' and press into the apples.

Bake in a moderate oven and baste the apples from time to time with the sauce in the dish. This will go tacky if you did not butter the dish freely.

Apple Dumpling

Paste to line a pudding bowl.

12 oz plain white flour
6 oz finely shredded suet
1 level teaspoonful baking
powder

A saltspoonful of salt
Cold water to mix to a firm
dough

Divide the dough into a large piece to fill the pudding bowl and a small piece for the lid. Keep the paste of an even thickness when rolling it out (it may break if you have a thinnish patch). Line the bowl carefully.

Peel, quarter and core 1 lb of cooking apples. Put half of them in the lined bowl and add 6 oz sugar. Add the rest of the apples, add a little more sugar, 2 tablespoonfuls of water with a little ground ginger mixed in it, and a teaspoonful of melted butter. Wet round the top of the paste, fit the lid on firmly and then cover with buttered paper. Tie a pudding cloth securely on top of the paper.

Cook steadily in a pan with a tight fitting lid for $2\frac{1}{2}$ hours. Do not let the water come more than half way up the bowl.

To serve, take it from the pan and leave it sitting for 5 minutes in a warm place before turning it out.

Apple Charlotte

Butter a pie dish freely. Line it carefully with quite thick pieces of bread also freely buttered. Cut the bread so that it lines the pie dish perfectly with no cracks or seams. Fill it with some cooked tart apples sweetened to taste and over them spread some raspberry jam. Now cover with soft white breadcrumbs into which you have mixed a spoonful of fine pounded sugar and a trace of ground cinnamon.

Moisten the crumbs well with run butter and then cover with more fine sugar and cinnamon.

Bake in a moderate oven until brown and crisp. The bread touching the pie dish should be crisp, too.

Apple Roly-Poly

½ lb flour
4 oz finely shredded suet

½ teaspoonful baking powder
and a pinch of salt

Filling

8 oz grated apple
4 oz currants

2 tablespoonfuls syrup
Grated nutmeg

First of all put on the pot in which you are going to boil the roly with a small plate in the bottom and half fill it with water. Next make the paste: sift the flour into the baking bowl, add the baking powder and the salt. Rub in the suet and mix to a firm dough with cold water. Roll out on a well floured board in a long strip, fairly thin. Spread the grated apples over it, leaving the edges clear, cover the apples with the currants and add a dust of grated nutmeg. Finally, trickle the syrup over it.

Damp the edges all round and roll up the paste very firmly, then pinch the edges to seal them securely. Scald a pudding cloth, tie the roll firmly but not too tightly, plump into the pan and boil steadily for 2½ hours.

Moray Apple Bake

Two lbs of cooking apples, pared, cored and cut up.

Infuse 4 cloves in 1 gill of water, take them out and melt 6 oz of sugar in it. Put the apples into a deep baking dish and pour the syrup over them. Top with 4 oz of sweet firm suet grated, 4 oz of soft brown sugar and 8 oz of not too fine oatmeal, and a handful of shelled hazel nuts chopped fine. Mix well together, scatter over the apples, shake another 4 oz of soft brown sugar on top.

Bake for 1 hour in a moderate oven. At least half of that time the apples should be at the boil and bubbling up.

Serve hot with a dish of whipped cream.

A 'Clootie' Dumpling

First, boil some water in a roomy pot with a saucer or a small plate in the bottom of it. Wring the pudding cloth out of very hot water and dust it with flour.

For the dumpling:

½ lb plain white flour	½ teaspoonful bicarbonate of
½ teaspoonful ground cinnamon	soda
½ teaspoonful mixed spice	A saltspoonful salt

should be put in a bowl, and to this add:

4 oz sugar	4 oz sultanas
4 oz finely shredded suet	1 tablespoonful treacle
4 oz currants	Milk

Use just enough milk to make a firm dough. Tidy into a ball, place in the centre of the pudding cloth and tie it up. Leave room for the dumpling to swell.

Drop it into the pan of boiling water and let it boil steadily for 2½ hours. Add more boiling water if necessary.

To turn out a 'clootie' dumpling, have a bowl that the dumpling will fit into easily and also a bowl of cold water. When you take the dumpling from the pan of boiling water, dip it, just for a second, into the bowl of cold water. If the dumpling is inclined to stick to the cloth these shock tactics will cure that. Now put it into the other bowl. Untie the string and fold back the pudding cloth; put an ashet over the bowl with the dumpling and invert it.

Grandmama's Pudding

12 oz soft white breadcrumbs	8 oz sultanas
4 oz plain white flour	4 oz finely shredded peel
1 teaspoonful mixed spice	8 oz syrup
A saltspoonful salt	4 oz butter
1 teaspoonful baking soda	Milk, if necessary

Sift the flour with the salt, spice and baking soda and add the crumbs and the fruit to it. Melt the syrup and the butter in a pan and work this into the pudding. It must be very moist: if necessary add a little milk at blood heat. Steam for 3 hours.

Serve with Caudle Sauce.

Jam Roly-Poly

Put on a pan with water and a plate in it. Wring a pudding cloth out of very hot water and dust it with flour.

½ lb flour
3 oz finely shredded suet
A pinch of salt

½ teaspoonful baking powder
Cold water to mix
Jam

Make a very firm paste with the flour, suet, baking powder and cold water. Roll it out evenly and smoothly into an oblong shape about ⅓ inch thick. Spread with a stiff jam (blackcurrant, apricot or plum), moisten round the edges with cold water and roll up. Seal the ends firmly and put the roly on the prepared cloth, roll it up in the cloth and tie the ends firmly. Leave a little room for swelling.

Drop it into the pot and keep it boiling for 2½ hours. Do not let it go off the boil. Unroll it quickly and slip it on a hot ashet when it is ready.

Colonel Cameron's Layer Pudding

8 oz plain white flour
2 tablespoonfuls soft white
  breadcrumbs
5 oz finely chopped suet
½ teaspoonful raising agent
  (baking powder)
Pinch of salt

Cold water to mix
6 tart cooking apples
4 tablespoonfuls golden syrup
4 tablespoonfuls grated or
  desiccated coconut
½ teaspoonful ground ginger

Make a firm paste with the flour, crumbs, suet, baking powder and water. Divide it into four pieces; one piece to line a pudding bowl, two for two layers, and one for a lid. Roll each piece to the desired size and of an even thickness. Line a well greased pudding bowl.

Peel the apples, core them and chop them up quickly so that the colour is not spoiled. Liquify the syrup, stir in the coconut and the ground ginger. Add the apples to this and mix well. Place a layer in the bottom of the bowl, put on a round of paste, then more mixture and another round. Add the last of the mixture and then put on the lid firmly.

Cover securely and steam in a pan of boiling water for 3 hours.

Fair Maids

(Colonel Cameron's recipe for a sweet to be taken to a lunch on the moors.)

1 quart sweet milk (new un-skimmed milk)	4 oz currants
	1 gill thick cream
2 dessertspoons rennet	½ gill brandy
2 eggs	Grated nutmeg
2 oz sugar	Shortcrust paste

Bring the milk to blood heat, stir in the rennet, and leave until quite set. When quite firm break it up and put it in a fine strainer to drain off the whey. Pick over the currants and rub in a towel to make sure they are absolutely clean. Beat the eggs with the sugar, stir in the curd, squeezed as dry as possible, then the cream, the currants and last the brandy and the nutmeg.

Roll out the paste and cut according to the size of your patty tins (4 inch if for a lunch on the moors, smaller if for a tea table). Fit a lining of paste into each tin bringing it well up to the top.

Fill three-quarters full with the mixture and bake in a moderately hot oven until an orange brown in colour (15-20 minutes according to size).

Lochnagar Steamed Pudding

4 oz plain white flour	½ teaspoonful ground ginger
4 oz soft white breadcrumbs	½ teaspoonful ground cinnamon
4 oz finely shredded suet	1 saltspoonful salt
4 oz soft brown sugar	4 oz, or more if you wish, of
1 large tablespoonful syrup	currants
½ teaspoonful bicarbonate of	1 heaped tablespoonful soft
soda	brown sugar

Grease a pudding bowl well and butter the bottom thickly. Put the sugar in and add the currants. Now mix the other ingredients together and make into a soft dough with a cupful of milk. Put the dough on top of the spoonful of sugar and currants and cover with a butter paper.

Tie down firmly with a pudding cloth and steam for 2 hours. Do not let it off the boil and add more water if necessary.

Her Majesty's Pudding

(Colonel Cameron's recipe, said to have come from Balmoral.)

This dish can be made for a dinner party along with caramel soufflé. Whisk the yolks of eight eggs with ½ pint of milk and 2 oz of finely sifted sugar until they are well broken. Add 1 pint pouring cream and season delicately with vanilla essence.

Butter a mould and pour in the mixture. Tie up securely and steam steadily for 30 minutes. Let it sit in the mould for a few minutes then turn it out on the dish on which you are to serve it. Decorate with apricot jam and serve hot or cold with pouring cream.

Meringues

The secret of a good meringue is a slow, but not too slow, oven. (If it is too cool the sugar will melt and run out of the mixture.) I like a cooling oven, pre-heated to 250°F and lowered to 200°F when the meringues are put in.

First, turn two baking sheets upside down and cover with smooth white kitchen paper well brushed with butter or sweet oil. Place 2 tablespoons in a jug of very cold water. Weigh out ½ lb of castor sugar and sift it. Break 3 whites of eggs, perfectly free from yolk, into a wide and shallow bowl. Beat the whites steadily until they are stiff and dry and can be lifted in a lump. Remove the whisk. Take a spoon and fold in (do not beat or stir) the sugar gradually until all the sugar is merged.

To shape the meringues take the spoons out of the cold water and shake them dry. With one spoon lift a portion of the mixture and with the other shape it neatly and scoop it out on to the buttered paper. Leave a slight space between each meringue. Go on until all the mixture is out, then very lightly dust each one with a shake of castor sugar.

Bake in the oven until quite firm (this will take 3 hours). Meringues keep for a long time if kept in an airtight tin. Two cases are put together with beaten, slightly sweetened and flavoured cream.

Colonel Cameron's Recipe for Caramel Soufflé

This quantity is for a 4 pint mould.

The whites of 8 eggs
6 oz finely sifted sugar
A few drops of an essence or a half teaspoonful finely grated lemon peel

Caramel
7 oz loaf sugar
½ gill water

Boil the loaf sugar with the water and keep stirring until it is a good dark colour. Line the soufflé tin with the caramel but on no account grease or butter the mould as the addition of a fat would change the character of the caramel. Beat the whites stiffly in a roomy basin and slowly fold in the sugar and the flavouring.

Fill into the prepared tin, cover securely and steam gently for ½ hour. The tin must not float. Remove from steamer and let it sit for five minutes. Turn it out on the dish on which you are to serve it and when quite cold sprinkle with finely chopped nuts.

Serve with whipped cream.

Note: I find that castor and icing sugar well sifted together give a lovely texture. At the time of this recipe vanilla pods were kept in the sugar jar and gave a very delicate flavour to either castor or icing sugar.

Mincemeat for Christmas Pies

1 lb Demerara sugar
1 lb currants
1 lb sultanas
1 lb muscatel raisins, stoned weight
1 lb suet finely chopped

1 lb apples, peeled, cored and chopped
4 oz finely shredded orange peel
4 oz finely shredded lemon peel
The juice of 3 lemons
A glass of brandy

Mix all the ingredients well; the muscatels should be cut up a little. Bottle and seal. Keep at least six weeks before using and stir from the bottom when you do start to make your pies.

Caudle Sauce

4 oz Demerara sugar or soft
  brown sugar
4 oz butter

½ wine glass of rum
A flavouring of ground
  cinnamon

Crush the sugar until it is powdered and then beat it with the butter until you have a creamy mixture. Work in the cinnamon and then gradually the rum. Add a little more rum if you think it requires it.

Serve with plum puddings, any fruit dumplings and apple pies.

Crême Brulée

This is an old Scots recipe, very much easier to make than of yore. Sir Arthur Farquhar and Sir James Ferguson both list it in a 1901 bazaar book as their favourite sweet. The top was bruléed with a salamander or as in the case of the recipe given to me, with an old iron saucepan heated until it was red hot.

5 yolks of eggs
1 pint single cream
A pinch of salt

A few drops of an essence
1 tablespoonful sugar
Sifted sugar for the topping

Beat the yolks in a roomy bowl then add the salt, essence and sugar and beat a little again. They should not be beaten to a froth. Bring the cream to the boil and pour over the eggs, beating the while.

Pour it into the dish in which it is to be served and set in a slow oven until quite set. Let it get cold, then heavily strew the top with sifted sugar. Brown under a great heat until the crust is a brittle golden top; it cannot be hurried.

Serve cold with pouring cream.

Miss Mary's Plum Pudding

This is an unusual recipe in which the mixture is made up, kept uncooked for a period and cooked on the day it is to be eaten.

1 lb suet	4 oz citron peel
1 lb fine white breadcrumbs	1 lb soft brown sugar
1 lb currants	4 oz sweet almonds
1 lb sultanas	1 teaspoonful salt
1 lb muscatel raisins	1 grated nutmeg
4 oz orange peel	The grated rind of 2 lemons
4 oz lemon peel	

Choose the suet with great care; it must be hard, firm and sweet smelling. Remove all skin and chop it very finely, dusting it with flour to keep it from clogging. Mix all the ingredients together and add $\frac{1}{2}$ pint of brandy. See that the mixture is really well mixed and then pack it closely into a very clean, very dry crock. Dip a piece of tissue paper in brandy and spread it firmly over the mixture. Cover again with greaseproof paper, then brown paper and tie down firmly.

Store in a really cold room.

To cook this pudding, take the required amount of mixture, according to the number to be catered for. To 1 lb of mixture allow 4 eggs, which should be well beaten and mixed into the pudding mixture.

Place it in a greased pudding bowl, tie it down and cook for 5 hours. It can also be boiled in a cloth.

Carry's Plum Pudding

A little unusual, but very good, recipe:

$\frac{1}{2}$ lb lard
$\frac{1}{2}$ lb castor sugar
1 large tablespoonful treacle
4 eggs
$\frac{1}{4}$ lb plain white flour
1 lb soft white breadcrumbs
$\frac{1}{2}$ lb grated carrot
A good glass of rum

1 lb currants
1 lb sultanas
1 lb blue raisins
1 lb mixed peel
$\frac{1}{2}$ teaspoonful salt
$\frac{1}{2}$ a nutmeg grated
1 teaspoonful mixed spice

Beat the lard and sugar to a cream and then beat in the treacle. Beat the eggs well and work them into the creamed mixture before working in the flour, the crumbs and then the rum. (Start adding the rum when the mixture gets stiffish). Work in the fruit and then the seasoning and add a little more rum if it will stand it.

Boil in a cloth or a pudding basin for 5 hours. Keep it at least a month before using. If you boil it in a cloth, put on a dry cloth when the pudding is quite cold and hang it up out of the dust.

Potato and Treacle Pudding: Mrs McLeod's

Cook the potatoes specially for this pudding and add just a suspicion of salt to the water. Shake them well until they are dry and mealy and then mash them until they are very smooth.

To $\frac{1}{2}$ lb of potato work in 4 oz of flour, 2 oz of soft white breadcrumbs and 3 oz of finely shredded suet. Add 3 tablespoonfuls of treacle and mix to a soft dough. Last, work in $\frac{1}{2}$ a teaspoonful of bicarbonate of soda. Put it through a sieve in case of lumps; then place it in a greased bowl and steam for 2 hours.

Colonel Cameron's Rice Pudding

4 oz best whole rice
1½ pints milk
1 tablespoonful sugar
A saltspoonful of salt
1 cup good cream

2 oz desiccated coconut, or a cupful of freshly grated coconut
Some double cream
Some slivers preserved ginger

Butter a fireproof dish thoroughly. Wash the rice, put it in the dish and add the milk, the salt and the sugar. Let this bake long and slowly until it looks like curry rice.

Soak the desiccated coconut overnight in the cream and add it to the cooked rice (take care not to mush the rice when adding the coconut).

When it is cold pile it into a glass bowl, top with lots of whipped cream and stick in the preserved ginger at odd points.

Making a Soufflé

The foundation of a soufflé must be firm and it is raised by well beaten egg yolks and whites. It is an improvement to add one white more than yolks.

There are attractive white china soufflé dishes, clear fireproof ones, both large and individual, but you can also use a cake tin or even a tinfoil case.

As a soufflé rises considerably it is necessary to prepare the tin or dish by tying a double band of greased paper round the top, giving an extra four inches in height. Butter the dish well. The usual foundation, or panada, is made with 1 oz butter, 1 oz flour, 1 gill liquid and 3 eggs.

Melt the butter in a saucepan, add the flour and then the liquid. Cook until the mixture leaves the sides of the pan cleanly. Add any other ingredients such as fish, meat or cheese, then the yolks beaten as stiff as possible and then the whites, also beaten stiff and folded into the mixture. If the soufflé is baked, the oven temperature must remain at an even 350°F. If steamed it must not go off the boil for an instant.

Lemon Soufflé

2 oz butter	3 eggs
2 oz flour	2 oz castor sugar
2 gills milk	Grated rind one lemon

Make the panada, add the sugar and the grated lemon rind and let it cool a little. Beat the yolks until they are light and foamy and add them; beat the whites until stiff and fold them in.

Pour into a prepared soufflé dish and bake for 40 minutes. It must be eaten as soon as it is taken from the oven. If left sitting, it will fall.

Steamed Vanilla Soufflé

Prepare the dish by greasing it well and adding the paper band round the top. Make a panada with:

1 oz flour	1 oz sugar
1 oz butter	Vanilla essence
1 gill milk	3 eggs

Pour into the prepared dish, cover with a greased paper and steam for 40 minutes. It must not go off the boil for a minute.

Sultana Dumpling

2 oz fine oatmeal	8 oz sultanas
2 oz plain white flour	1 heaped teaspoonful baking
2 oz grated soft white bread-	powder
crumbs	A saltspoonful of salt
2 oz finely shredded suet	Milk to mix
4 oz sugar	

Mix all the ingredients together and mix to a soft dough with milk. It should be of a dropping consistency (it should drop easily from the spoon).

Put into a greased pudding bowl, cover, and steam for 2½ hours.

This used to be a 'clootie dumpling' and was boiled for 2 hours in a pudding cloth.

Carry's Yule Pudding

½ lb soft white breadcrumbs
½ lb plain white flour
½ lb finely shredded suet
½ lb raisins
½ lb sultanas
½ lb currants
½ lb mixed peel

½ lb soft brown sugar
Juice and rind of 1 lemon
½ a nutmeg grated
1 teaspoonful mixed spice
½ teaspoonful salt
1 tablespoonful treacle
4 eggs

Stone the raisins, wash and pick over the currants and the sultanas. Shred the peel. Grate the lemon and squeeze it. Beat the eggs thoroughly. Mix the flour, the crumbs, the suet and the sugar into a roomy mixing basin. Add the flavouring, then the fruit, the eggs, the lemon juice and the treacle to make a moist mixture: if it should be stiff add a little milk.

Scald a pudding cloth, dust it heavily with flour and put the pudding into it (this is easier to do if you have the scalded cloth in a bowl). Tie it securely and drop it into a pan of boiling water with a plate in the bottom.

Boil steadily for 4 hours. It mellows if kept for some time before using. The day after it is boiled, remove the damp cloth and put on a dry one.

Jams, Jellies, Pickles and Herbs

Jam

The condition of fruit for jam is important: it should be ripe and firm but not over-ripe, as over-ripe fruit is difficult to set. Fruits which are rich in pectins and acids jell easily (in fact it is the pectin and acid which controls the jellying power when cooked with sugar). Pectin forms as the fruit ripens, and commences to break down as the fruit passes perfection. Fruits like gooseberries, currants, plums and sharp apples are rich in pectin, which is why some sharp juice, such as red currant juice is added to strawberries and other fruits that are lacking in it. Lemon juice, tartaric acid and acetic acid serve the same purpose.

There is a jellying point in jams and jellies and if you are lucky enough to catch it then your jams and jellies will have a lovely clear colour, a delicious flavour and the right texture. Over-boiling breaks down pectin and thus long boiled jam or jelly can be very difficult to set. It is impossible to say exactly how long jam or jelly will take to set: there are too many factors such as the condition of the fruit. The sugar, too, can make some little difference.

Start testing for jellying after 15 minutes boiling by putting a little in a saucer and set it in a cool place. If it crinkles when you tilt the saucer it is ready to lift. Some are guided by the jam spoon; if the juice begins to hang like crystal drops to the jam spoon when you hold it up, it is certainly ready for lifting.

All fruit must be as clean as it can be made. Firm fruit like plums, damsons, apples, gooseberries should be washed and left to dry in a sieve or colander, or even on a large dish cloth or towel. Fruit with stones should have them removed but some kept to cook them with the jam. There is much divided opinion about washing strawberries. I like to hull them into a deep colander and then dip the colander rapidly up and down in a basin of water; after that I let them sit for at least two hours to drip. I also like to cover strawberries with sugar and leave them overnight: this gives a good syrup to start with and there is less risk of the jam burning.

If you want to add a juice to a fruit in order to help the jam to set the best is red currant juice. It has a high pectin content and a delicious flavour, which does not intrude. To 2 lb of red currants add ½ pint of water and set it by a slow heat to draw all the juice. Strain it well. This should be sufficient for 7 lb of fruit. Allow sugar for the quantity of juice. Tartaric acid goes well with vegetable marrow, cherries and grapefruit. Allow ½ oz of tartaric acid to 8 lb of fruit or 1 small level teaspoonful to 2 lb of fruit. To make juice for jellying I use the old fashioned method of just covering the fruit and no more with cold water. Currants must be stripped from the stalks, apples cut in very thin slices with peel and core left on. All fruit must be cooked to a pulp and left in the jelly bag to drip all night.

Most fruits take equal amounts of sugar, that is, pound for pound. Cherries with the stones in, or any other fruit with stones do not require the equal amount, 12 oz to the pound of fruit is sufficient. The jellying time should be anything from 15 to 25 minutes.

A tiny knob of butter is an improvement in any jam as it keeps excessive scum from forming and as all jam must be well skimmed during the boiling process the butter will certainly be skimmed off.

Black Currant Jam

6 lb black currants   9 lb sugar
3 pints of water   1 oz butter

Wash the berries and tail them (it is not necessary to top them).
Put them into the jam pan with the water, and bring to the boil:
allow to boil gently for 20 minutes then add the sugar and the
butter. Bring back to the boil and skim occasionally. Test for setting
after 15 minutes boiling.

Gooseberry Jam

7 lb gooseberries   Water
9 lb sugar

Wash and tail the berries and put them into the jam pan. Just cover
them and no more with water, bring to the boil and let them cook
for 30 minutes.

Add the sugar and a tiny piece of butter and let it boil quite
briskly for 15 minutes, skimming occasionally. Then start to test
for setting.

Strawberry and Gooseberry Jam

Equal quantities of strawberries and gooseberries and sugar equal
to the weight of the two fruits.

Hull the strawberries and dip them for a second in cold water.
Leave them to drip. Top and tail the gooseberries and put them
into the jam pan. Add just enough water to keep them from
sticking and cook them until they are tender. Add the sugar and
the strawberries and bring to the boil again. Boil steadily and begin
to test for a set after 20 minutes cooking.

Rhubarb Jam

| 6 lb rhubarb | 8 lb sugar |
| 3 lb plums | |

Cook the plums in sufficient water to cover them. Wash, dry and cut up the rhubarb in 1 inch pieces. Put the rhubarb into the jam pan, the sugar over it and add the plum juice. Leave overnight. Cook gently for 1 hour.

Marrow Marmalade

3 lb prepared weight of vege-	1 oz root ginger
table marrow	Juice of 2 lemons
3 lb cooking apples	Sugar

Wash the apples and slice them into the jam pan; add the marrow seeds. Thinly slice the lemons and add them; bruise the ginger with the tattie chapper, add it and just enough water to cover this mixture, and bring to the boil. Cook until the apples are soft, put into the jelly bag and leave hanging overnight.

Next day put the juice and the marrow diced together and measure it. Allow 1 lb of sugar to 1 pint of pulp and bring to the boil. Boil until it sets: it may take an hour, depending on the jellying properties of the apples.

Plum Jam

| 6 lb plums | 1½ pints water |

If the stones are not removed 5 lb of sugar will be sufficient. If the fruit is stoned, weight for weight of pulp and sugar, and ½ lb over. Cook for 30 minutes and test for set after that.

Apple and Grapefruit Jam

12 oz grapefruit   2 lb sugar
2 lb cooking apples   1½ pints water

Put the whole grapefruits into a pan with the water and cook them gently until the peel seems soft, keeping the water up to 1½ pints. When quite cooked cut the fruit in half, scoop out the pulp and remove the pips. Cut the peel into tiny chunks. Peel, core and cut the apples into slivers, and cook in the juice in which the grapefruit was cooked. Now add the peel, the pulp and the sugar. Bring to the boil and let it boil until it gells (usually 20 minutes).

Apricot and Apple Jam

This is a very old recipe belonging to the days of greenhouses with apricots on the walls and is a delicious preserve.

Take equal quantities of apples and apricots, say 2 lb of a good jellying apple and 2 lb of whole apricots (without the stones). Wash the apples and cut them up finely. Put them into the jam pan, just cover with cold water, and cook until soft. If you are using fresh apricots add some of the stones, broken open, to the apple mixture. Wash and stone the apricots (if dried they must be well washed). Cut them in half and put them into an earthenware basin. Hang the jelly bag over it and pour in the apple pulp. Leave to drip and let the apricots sit for 24 hours in the juice before cooking.

Measure it and add 1 lb of sugar to each pint of fruit. Boil until it sets: much depends on the quality of the apples so test after 20 minutes boiling.

Blackcurrant Jelly

Blackcurrants that are just ripening are the best for this (if they are very ripe and juicy the pectin in the fruit is already beginning to break down). Wash the currants and put them into the jam pan; barely cover with cold water and bring slowly to the boil. Bruise the fruit as much as possible.

When it is thoroughly pulped and the juice very free lift into the jelly bag and leave to drip overnight. To every pint of juice allow 1 lb of sugar. Bring the juice to the boil before adding the sugar. Stir until the sugar melts and the jelly comes to the boil. Skim if necessary (the pure clear colour of any jelly depends on skimming in the early stages). It jellies quickly, usually in about 5 minutes.

Red Currant Jelly (no water)

Pick over the currants and put them into a wide necked jar. Set the jar in a pan of boiling water and keep this boiling gently, adding more water if necessary. Stir the fruit and bruise it with a wooden spoon from time to time. It is a long slow process but well worth it. When you think all the juice is free strain through muslin (not flannel as this retains too much of the juice) leaving it hanging overnight. To every pint of juice allow 1 lb of sugar.

Bring quickly to the boil and test for set after 5 minutes. It jells almost at once.

Gooseberry and Mint Jelly

4 lb green gooseberries
A small bunch of mint
1 tablespoonful white vinegar

1 lb sugar to 1 pint juice
3 pints water

Put the gooseberries on with the water and add the mint cut up a little. Cook to a pulp and then add the vinegar. Cook for 5 minutes and then strain through the jelly bag. Measure the juice and add sugar in the proportion of a pound to a pint of juice. Put back into the jelly pan, colour a little with green colouring and bring to the boil.

Boil steadily until it jells, usually quite quickly. Pot in small pots and cover when cold.

Bramble and Apple Jelly

2 lb good jellying apple (even crab apples)

6 lb brambles
Sugar

Pick over the brambles. Wash the apples and cut into small pieces without paring them. Put the brambles and the apples into the preserving pan and just cover with water and no more. Stir until the mixture comes to the boil and then boil gently stirring from time to time until the whole is reduced to pulp. Allow to drip overnight in the jelly bag.

Next day measure the juice, put it into the pan and add 1 lb of sugar for every pint of juice. Bring to the boil and let it boil quite briskly for 15 minutes, skimming from time to time, and from that time test with a little in a saucer. If it wrinkles at a touch of the finger, it is ready for pouring.

Pot and cover it when it is quite cold.

Arbuthnott House Raspberry Jam

(A recipe used in that kitchen about 1894.)

2 lb fresh, dry raspberries	½ pint red currant juice
3 lb sugar	A nut of butter

Make the juice by barely covering red currants with cold water and boiling them until mushy. Drip. Heat the butter in the jam pan, enough to melt it, add the juice and the sugar and stir until it comes to the boil.

Add the raspberries and bring to the boil again. Boil for 5 minutes only. Skim, let the jam sit for about 10 minutes away from the heat: then pot. Cover when cold.

Lemon Curd

1 lemon	2 eggs
1 oz butter	4 oz sugar

Grate the rind off the lemon; then squeeze the lemon and strain the juice. Beat the eggs well and put them through a strainer to remove any 'strings'. Put the ingredients into a bowl and set the bowl in a pan of boiling water and stir until the mixture coats the spoon. The mixture itself must not come through the boil.

Put into little pots and cover when cold.

Marrow Jam

Peel, core and finely dice a marrow until you have 5 lb of prepared fruit. Add the juice and grated rind of 3 lemons, and ½ oz of bruised root ginger tied in a piece of muslin. Cover with 4 lb of sugar and leave overnight.

Cook until it sets (usually in about 45 minutes).

Note: A very old recipe gives crystallised ginger cut up finely and three cayenne pods to this amount of lemon and marrow.

Red Currant Jelly with Water

Make exactly as for blackcurrant jelly.

Raspberry Jelly

This jelly is perfect in taste and colour when made without water being added to the fruit. Put the raspberries into a wide necked jar or even a bowl and set it in boiling water in the jam pan. Mash down the fruit and leave to 'draw'. When you feel the juice is free strain overnight in muslin. Allow 1 lb of sugar to 1 pint of juice and test for setting in 4 minutes.

Raspberry Jelly with Red Currants

Take 2 lb of red currants to 5 lb of raspberries and to this add 2 pints of water. Boil together, making sure the red currants are broken down and all the juice extracted. Strain. Use 1 lb of sugar to 1 pint of juice. Test for jellying after 10 minutes boiling.

Cranberry Jelly

Pick over the berries, place them in the preserving pan and add water to cover half the berries (to cover them completely would be too much and ruin the jellying properties). Bring slowly to the boil, bruising the fruit as much as possible, and when pulpy strain through fine muslin and leave to drip overnight.

Allow 1 lb of sugar to 1 pint of juice. Boil briskly until it jells, testing from time to time. Pot in small pots. This jelly is excellent with game.

Strawberry Jam

Hull the berries into a colander. Dip the colander quickly two or three times into a basin of clean cold water, then let the colander sit to drip for an hour.

Weigh the fruit and put it into the jam pan with 1 lb of sugar to each pound of berries and leave overnight. Place the sugar and fruit in the pan in layers. This gives a syrup to begin with. Stir until the fruit comes to the boil and boil briskly until the jam sets, usually from 25 to 35 minutes.

Strawberry jam needs a good deal of skimming but this can be cut by putting in a small piece of butter. This also lessens the risks of boiling over.

To Re-boil Jam or Jelly

If for some reason, perhaps mould or a bad set, you have to re-boil jam or jelly this is a good method because it prevents you losing perhaps 2 lb of your jam or jelly in the re-boiling.

If mould is the trouble, take very good care to remove it all before re-boiling. Slice 2 lb of a good cooking apple, skins, core and all, and just cover them with cold water. Cook to a pulp and strain through the jelly bag. Measure the juice. You should have about 1½ pints. Allow sugar in the usual proportion, 1 lb of sugar to 1 pint of juice.

Put the juice and the sugar into the jam pan and boil for 5 minutes before adding the jam or jelly to be re-boiled. Boil until you get a good set.

The Pickle Jar
Spiced Vinegar

Buy spices for pickling whole. To make spiced vinegar, allow 2 oz whole mixed spices to 1 quart bottle of vinegar. There is no hard and fast rule as to flavour and you can omit any flavour you dislike. You can infuse vinegar with spices by bringing it slowly to the boil with the spices in it and letting it simmer for 15 minutes before straining it, or you can simply put the spices in the bottle of vinegar, cork it well and leave it for at least six weeks before using.

If the vinegar is to be used for pickling vegetables some of the spices such as pods and peppercorns can be left in the jar with the vegetables, but never clove as they give a very strong flavour to any vegetable with which they come in contact. For chutneys and sauces the vinegar must be strained.

Carrot Pickle

Carrot pickle is not only good to eat but lends an attractive note of colour to any dish.

Cook the required number of carrots, young ones for preference, and cut them into dice. Put them into jars, bring the required amount of spiced vinegar to the boil and pour the boiling liquid over them. Seal when cold. Never leave spices in a carrot pickle as carrots discolour easily.

Beetroot

Do beetroot in the same way, taking care not to bruise the skin of the beet before cooking. Any bruising or cuts will cause beets to 'bleed' and ruin their colour. For beetroot allow 2 oz of sugar to a quart of vinegar.

A Preserve to serve with Venison

3 lb green gooseberries   3 pints water
6 to 8 oz fresh green parsley   5 lb sugar

Wash the parsley thoroughly. Put the parsley, gooseberries and water into the jam pan and boil gently until the berries are into pulp. Pour into the straining bag and leave to hang over a wide bowl overnight.

Next day return the juice to the pan, add the sugar, boil briskly, and test from time to time. It should jell in about 20 minutes.

Gooseberry Chutney

Top and tail 2 lb of gooseberries. Parboil 1 large onion or 2 or 3 small ones and chop up small. Put a quart of spiced vinegar into a pan, add the gooseberries, the onion and 2 lb of sugar. Cook until very nearly ready then add 1 lb of raisins which have been soaked in warm water overnight. The chutney must cook for at least 10 minutes after the raisins have been added.

Pot, and seal when quite cold.

STRENGTH, VIGOUR, and PLUCK !

CADBURY's Cocoa is world-renowned for its absolute purity, and its strengthening and sustaining properties. The highest compliments have been paid to it: NANSEN and JACKSON selected it for their famous Polar Expeditions; and the Medical Profession and all expert judges accord it unstinted praise.

CADBURY's Cocoa is Absolutely Pure, and a "PERFECT FOOD."

Chutney: The Admiral's Choice

Note. This is a hot chutney, and a very personal taste, so do not add all the salt or all the cayenne until half way through the cooking when you can taste it and judge for yourself. Bought mustard can be used, the mustard mentioned here was pounded in an old iron pot kept for that purpose.

2 lb sharp cooking apples	2 teaspoonfuls ground ginger
2 lb under-ripe tomatoes	2 teaspoonfuls ground mustard
1 lb pickling onions	seed
1 lb sultanas	2 teaspoonfuls curry powder
1 lb Demerara sugar	1 heaped tablespoonful capers
2 pints vinegar	2 oz salt
2 teaspoonfuls cayenne pepper	2 pints vinegar

Wash the sultanas and just leave barely covered with water overnight. They should 'drink' all the water: if not, put the remainder into the chutney. Peel, core and cut up the apples; dice the onions and tomatoes. If the latter are pretty green do not trouble about the skin but if they will peel, plump them for a second into boiling water and peel. Mix all the dry spices through and through the sugar.

Put the vinegar into a jam pan, add all the other ingredients, and stir until it comes to the boil. Cook gently for 1 hour.

Pickled Cabbage

Red cabbage is the variety used in pickling, but savoys also make an excellent pickle. Use freshly gathered cabbage and trim off the coarse leaves. Cut in four lengthwise and remove any very hard core. Shred finely and put in layers into a crock or earthenware basin and sprinkle with salt, allowing 4 oz of salt to 1 lb of cabbage. Leave for two days, turning the cabbage occasionally. Drain very well.

Pack loosely into wide-necked jars, cover with spiced vinegar and seal. Keep for some weeks before using.

Clove Apples

These go well with pork or ham. They can be made like a chutney or can be kept in quarters.

4 lb apples	2 lb sugar
1 pint water	Cloves

Make a syrup with the water and the sugar. Peel, quarter and core the apples. Put them into the pan of syrup and cook until tender. At this stage you can decide to keep them in quarters or you can break them down.

When cooked lift the apples out of the syrup and put them into jars. Put the syrup back on the stove, add 2 cloves for every apple used and bring to the boil. Let this simmer for 20 minutes then strain over the apples.

Leave overnight to cool, then seal.

Apple and Mint Jelly

2 lb cooking apples	2 tablespoonfuls white vinegar
1½ pints water	to the pint
1 lb sugar to 1 pint juice	Colouring
2 tablespoonfuls chopped mint	
to the pint	

Cut up the apples into small pieces and put them into a jam pan with the water. Cook to a pulp and strain overnight. Measure the juice and put it into a pan; add the sugar. Strip the mint from the stalks and chop it up finely. Put the pan on the heat and stir until it comes to the boil: boil for 5 minutes. Add the mint and the vinegar and a few drops of green colouring and stir until the jelly sets. It usually sets easily.

Pour into small pots and seal when cold.

Pickled Onions

Choose small even-sized onions and peel them. Drop them into a pan of boiling water, give them about five minutes in it, drain them and bottle them. Cover with boiling spiced vinegar.

Ginger Apples

Ginger apples 'marry' well with cold roast mutton, any sausage mixture and rabbit.

4 oz root ginger	2 pints water
1 lemon	1 lb sugar
1 inch of cinnamon stick	4 lb apples, prepared weight

Bruise the root ginger, put it into a saucepan and add the water. Add the rind, the juice of the lemon and the cinnamon stick and simmer gently for 30 minutes. If it should boil in keep it up to 2 pints. Strain it, put it back into the pan and add the sugar and the apples, peeled and quartered.

Cook until the apples are tender, lift into jars and pour the syrup over them. Seal when cold.

Mushroom Ketchup

Mushrooms for a ketchup must be picked on a very dry day otherwise it will not keep. Seven pounds is a good working quantity. Take a sharp knife and trim off the end of the stalk and remove any discoloured part. It is not necessary to peel them. With the fingers break them up, stalks and all, into a large earthenware crock, sprinkling them with salt. Allow ½ lb for this quantity of mushrooms.

Cover with muslin and put the dish in a cool larder. Leave for three days but stir at least three times every day, using a silver spoon if possible. Place them in a preserving pan or an earthenware cooking pot, put on a slow heat and cook until you have a good supply of juice. Put into a muslin bag and hang up to drip. Shake the bag from time to time to help drainage but on no account squeeze them.

Measure the juice and put in a jar that will stand the heat. To every quart of liquid add 20 peppercorns put through a mill or beaten, ½ oz of bruised ginger, two blades of mace and a few grains of cayenne pepper. Cover the jar, set it in a pot of boiling water and let it boil for 2½ hours. Strain at least twice through cloth and bottle when cold. Well corked it keeps a long time.

16

Sauce Piquant

1 oz flour
1 oz castor sugar
1 tablespoonful treacle
½ teaspoonful salt

½ teaspoonful mixed spice
1 teaspoonful mustard
Quart of vinegar

Mix the dry ingredients together to a paste with a little cold water. Add the treacle and the vinegar. If you have a double saucepan, use it; if not, set the bowl with the mixture into a pan of boiling water and keep on stirring until the sauce coats the back of the spoon. Taste it and see if it will take a little more salt.

Bottle but do not cork until quite cold.

Tomato Sauce

Take any number of fresh, sound tomatoes and cut them in thin slices. Put them into an earthenware bowl and sprinkle a liberal coating of salt over them. Leave them a night, then cook to a pulp. Sieve the pulp and measure it. Return it to the pan and season in the following proportions. To every 4 pints of tomato puree:

1 teaspoonful mustard
1 teaspoonful ground ginger
1 teaspoonful ground clove

1 teaspoonful ground cinnamon
3 tablespoonfuls sugar
½ pint vinegar

Mix all the dry ingredients together, add the vinegar slowly and finally pour the mixture into the tomato puree. Bring to the boil and let the sauce simmer for 15 minutes. Taste and add more salt or sugar if you think it needs it. Bottle and cork when it is quite cold.

Vegetable Marrow Pickle

To 4 pints of vinegar add:

2 tablespoonfuls mustard	3 oz root ginger
1 oz turmeric	3 teaspoonfuls salt
12 peppercorns	½ lb sugar
1 blade of mace	1 large onion
1 inch of cinnamon stick	

Put the vinegar into a jam pan or lined saucepan and add the other ingredients; bruise the root ginger and slice the onion. Boil gently, just infusing and no more, for 30 minutes.

Meanwhile pare the marrow. Carefully remove the core and cut the flesh into cubes. Strain the vinegar and return it to the pan. Add the marrow and cook it until it is quite soft.

Put into wide-necked jars and cover when quite cold.

Piccalilli

To 1 quart of spiced vinegar add:

1 large teaspoonful cornflour	1 teaspoonful ground ginger
1 oz mustard powder	2 teaspoonfuls salt
1 oz turmeric powder	2 oz sugar

The vegetables used may be shallots, cauliflower, tomatoes, small onions, runner beans, carrot, vegetable marrow and cucumber.

Wash the vegetables. Sprig the cauliflower; peel the marrow and cut into chunks; do not peel the cucumber, but cut it into thickish slices and quarter: string the beans and cut into strips; peel the onions and leave them whole; peel the tomatoes, cut the peeled carrots in chunks. Parboil all the vegetables except the tomatoes in very salt water. Strain the vegetables well and pack into wide-necked jars.

Bring the vinegar to the boil with all the ingredients in it and pour over the vegetables. They must be quite covered. Seal securely when cold.

DRINKING THE BRIDE'S HEALTH
IN

JOHN ROBERTSON & SONS' DUNDEE WHISKY.
London Address: 4, GREAT TOWER ST., E.C.

Spiced Black Currants

A relish to serve with venison or black cock.

1 pint wine vinegar
1 lb preserving sugar
4 cloves

4 inches cinnamon stick
1 quart blackcurrants

Put the cloves and cinnamon stick broken up in shreds into a piece of muslin. Pour the vinegar into a suitable pan, add the spices and bring slowly to the boil. If it boils in at all keep it to the correct proportion. Add the sugar, stir until it melts and then bring the syrup to the boil. Boil gently for fifteen minutes skimming if necessary. Remove the muslin with the spices. Have the berries stripped from the stalks, tail but do not top them. Wash them well and allow to drip. Go over them for any deformed berries, etc., and then put into the boiling syrup.

Cook for 15 minutes over a low heat, stirring most of the time. Allow to cool a little before potting.

Rowan Liqueur

Take two handfuls of ripe red rowan berries and separate each berry from the stalk. Lay them on a sheet of paper in a sunny window until they are quite shrivelled up.

Put them in a wide-necked bottle and cover with 1 pint of brandy. Leave for ten or twelve days then strain off the berries and mix the brandy with an equal quantity of thick clear syrup, made with the best quality loaf sugar.

Bottle the liqueur and seal. Leave at least six months.

Rowan Jelly

To 3 lb of cooking apples allow 3 lb of rowan berries after they are off the stalks (pick them as red as possible). Cut up the apples into thin slices, put in the jam pan, add the rowan berries, and just cover with water. Boil to a pulp and put in the jelly bag to drip. Measure the juice and allow 1 lb of sugar to each pint of juice.

Pour the juice into a jam pan (an enamel pan is the best for this or of course the brass jelly pan), bring to the boil, add the sugar, and stir until it melts, and comes to the boil again. Skim if necessary and boil until it jells. Test for jelling on a cold plate after 15 minutes boiling.

Pot in smallish pots. Rowan jelly is excellent as a relish with game or venison.

Note: If possible use crab apples.

Spiced Bramble Jelly

6 lb brambles, not over ripe   1½ pints water
3 lb sharp cooking apples or   1 oz root ginger
   crab apples

Cook to a pulp and strain through the jelly bag. Allow 1 lb of sugar to each pint of juice and to the above quantities allow 1 level teaspoonful of ground cloves, ground mace and ground cinnamon. Mix the dry spices well through the sugar before adding to the juice. Boil until setting point. Pot in smallish pots.

Herbs

In Scotland it is never easy to harvest pot herbs in perfect condition and, perhaps for this very reason, they have never been widely used. Parsley, chives, mint and sage are the range of almost any kitchen garden with perhaps a laurel bush to supply leaves to flavour sauces and milk puddings. In the hedgerows is the Umbelliferae plant, the caraway, which gives us caraway seeds which at one time were used to flavour many Scots dishes, cakes and cheeses; myrrh used to flavour game. There is, however, such a wide range of herbs on the market now that a word about them may not be untimely.

Parsley

Parsley is the best known and most widely used herb. It is better when used fresh and not dried. Not only does it lend colour and decoration to many dishes, and flavour to soups, sauces, and stuffings, it is in itself a valuable herb being a source of some vitamins and iron. A preserve of a honey-like quality can also be made with parsley.

Mint

Mint is used to make mint sauce, mint jelly and to flavour green peas, pea and lentil soups, and new potatoes. Used sparingly it is good in salads and salad dressing.

Sage

Sage has a rather strong flavour and should be used with care. It 'marries' well with onion in a stuffing for poultry, particularly goose, and also with pork.

Bouquet Garni

A bouquet garni is a few sprigs of some herbs tied together in a piece of muslin and cooked with the food. They are discarded after the required flavour is obtained. A simple bouquet is made up of a spray of parsley, a sprig of thyme and a bay leaf. A bouquet garni is more elaborate with 2 sprays of parsley, 2 sprigs of thyme, a piece of bruised celery, a bay leaf, a sprig of rosemary and a sprig of marjoram.

Fennel

Fennel seeds suggest anise in flavour. Perhaps their most useful function is flavouring sweet pickles. A few fennel seeds give a distinctive flavour to cooked apples and pears. Be careful to remove the seeds before serving as they are not attractive when cooked.

Tarragon

Tarragon is best known as a flavouring for vinegar, and is also excellent in marinades.

Saffron

It has been said that saffron is to cooking as Chanel is to my lady's toilette, but it is little used today, perhaps because of its cost. It is useful for colouring cooked rice, fish soups, and for adding a rich colour to cakes.

Marjoram

Marjoram is a pungent herb and should be used with care. It can be used to advantage in soups, some stews and it is definitely an improvement in pork and sausage dishes. Just a suggestion of it is also good in stuffings for fish and poultry.

Rosemary

Rosemary is best when it is still green. It goes well with 'young' meats such as lamb, veal and chicken. A few sprigs in the roasting tin gives a most tantalising flavour to chicken.

Thyme

Thyme is pungent and aromatic and is at its best in a bouquet garni.

Dill

Dill is used in sprays but it is better known for its seeds which are used to flavour vinegar and pickles. Dill seeds remind one a little of caraway.

INDEX